Contents

I. Introduction

"We live in a box of space and time. Movies are windows in its walls. They allow us to enter other minds, not simply in the sense of identifying with the characters, although that is an important part of it, but by seeing the world as another person sees it."

Robert Egert, American film critic, author, journalist and historian (1942 – 2013)

Movies do not only allow us to enter other minds but also other cultures. Since learning a foreign language always implies understanding its foreign culture(s), movies can be seen as windows at the edge of the English classroom through which we can experience the other language and culture. Clint Eastwood's Gran Torino (2008) offers us insights into the lives of two people in Detroit who could hardly be more different from each other: Walt Kowalski, a racist, aging war veteran struggling with the burdens of his past, and his next-door neighbor Thao van Lor, an introvert Asian-American teenager searching for his identity and a sense of belonging.

These two protagonists face challenges that reflect some facets of the all-American experience: prejudices and racism, individualism and masculinity, violence and justice.

The aim of this book is to provide you with tasks and questions, information and tips through which to the explore various themes of the movie. As well as the study tips in the introduction and a helpful synopsis of the film, the book includes all the worksheets your teacher might use in your lessons. They are divided into three parts:

- Part I offers you an introduction to films in general and to *Gran Torino* in particular.
- Part II (Modul A) provides material for several project groups, who each then deal with different themes that are central to the movie *(Prejudices and racism; Masculinity, The Gran Torino* (i.e. the car itself), *Violence;* and *finally Religion).*
- The third part (Modul B) puts the focus on "the ambiguity of belonging" – the special subject for students in Baden-Wuerttemberg[1].

Your teacher might opt for the broader approach of module A, or the in-depth approach of module B or (s)he might combine tasks from both sections. Either way you can profit from *all* the material in this book, even from the worksheets that you do not use in class, since they give hints and raise questions that will help you gain a deeper understanding of the movie as a piece of cinematography and as a mirror of the American culture.

To all Abitur students in Baden-Wuerttemberg:

At first it might be difficult to grasp the meaning of the phrase "the ambiguity of belonging". The topic appears vague and ambiguous in itself, as it captures more a feeling than a matter of *fact:* We could ask ourselves: *"Who* exactly feels that (s)he belongs or does not belong to *who* or *what?"* Yet it is this very complexity that makes the topic so fascinating and rewarding as it applies to many aspects of our lives: our personal identities, our social bonds, our national and cultural identities.

The first and foremost aim of module B is to thoroughly prepare you for your English "Abiturklausur". With the help of the task sheets, you will be encouraged to explore the meanings of the phrase "the ambiguity of belonging": What does it mean to belong or not to belong (for different people in different situations)? Why is a sense of belonging so important to humans? How is our identity connected to the need to belong? What happens if we do not know where we belong? This thematic lead-in (B1 – B4) is accompanied by a focus on language (B5) that will help you to to express your observations and thoughts on this topic.

---

[1] Literarisches Schwerpunktthema in Baden-Württemberg ab Abitur 2019. Pflichtkanon: Tom Franklins Roman *Crooked Letter, Crooked Letter* und Clint Eastwoods *Gran Torino.*

To examine the different aspects of the topic "the ambiguity of belonging", we have selected a number of film sequences for you to work with. The task sheets (B7 – B13) are clearly structured and help you **understand** the film on these different levels:

- the plot (WHAT is happening?)
- the film techniques (What effect does the film have on the viewer and HOW is it created?)
- the film as a product of its culture(s) (What cultural concepts and values does the film mirror?).

In order to expand your vocabulary so that you feel more comfortable speaking or writing about the movie, there are "chunk boxes" on each task sheet that provide you with useful words and idiomatic phrases ("chunks" = pieces of language) for each scene. In addition to this, the language sheets from module A (A1.L – A5.L) cover the most important word fields that come up in the movie. It is definitely worth working with these language sheets, especially since all the themes overlap with the topic of "the ambiguity of belonging". You can also do this on your own – the solutions for all language sheets are included in this book (-> p. 75).

II. Understanding movies in English

1. Viewing tips

First make a guess at how many movies have you ever watched in your life. Now add to that number all the episodes of all the series that you have watched on TV, DVD or streaming media. No matter if you are an excessive or a more moderate film consumer – you already are a film expert: You know what you can expect from different film genres such as comedy, drama, action adventures or romances. You have learned to puzzle the story of a film together even if the movie leaves out important information or if the story jumps between two periods in time or between different plots that do not seem to be connected at first. You understand that intense music is often an indication that something dramatic is about to happen, and perhaps you are sometimes even able to predict what a character is about to do or say. So even though you might not be directly aware of this, you are already impressively competent at watching films. This is why you will easily master many of the challenges that you might face when watching a movie in English

Comprehension gaps

Don't get frustrated when you do not fully understand all the dialogues, you will still be able to follow the movie. You can get clues from the non-verbal communication (body language, facial expressions, voice quality, etc.) and of course from the action that you see. As a non-native speaker, it is normal that some dialogues are hard to understand, especially if there are several speakers, (some of) who may also have an accent, use slang expressions or speak extremely fast, or if there is a lot of background noise. Jokes are usually tough to understand in a foreign language, because they often refer to specific cultural phenomena you might not be familiar with.

English subtitles

If you watch a movie with English subtitles, be aware that you will be practicing *reading* not *listening*. For most people, reading is easier than listening. In addition, our eyes are always drawn to things that are moving. So it is hard to not read the subtitles if they are switched on. If you are watching the movie at home, you can switch the English subtitles on and off, for instance make them visible for certain scenes which are harder to understand but are central to understanding what's going on. Once you have understood the dialogue, watch the scene again *without* subtitles.

Sometimes it is difficult to understand what is going on at the beginning of a movie. Before you give up completely, switch on the English subtitles for a while, but then switch them off again as soon as you have gotten the gist of the story. Subtitles distract you from the actual, full viewing experience, because you won't be able to really pay attention to the visual qualities of the movie (camera operations, composition, lighting, colors, etc.) when your eyes are focused on the words at the bottom of the screen.

Unknown words

Of course you do not have to understand every single word, but if there are certain unknown words or expressions that recur, it might be a good idea to look them up. In *Gran Torino*, for example, the words 'confession' and 'confess' (meaning *Beichte/Geständnis* and *beichten/gestehen*) are used nine times in the course of the movie. 'Toad' (meaning *Kröte*) also occurs nine times – Walt banters with it; it is his (nick)name for Thao. "Salvation" (in German: *Erlösung*) is used four times.

Some of the words you probably do not know in *Gran Torino* are racial slurs, i.e. racist expressions that Walt Kowalski and his friends use frequently. Asian-Americans are called "swamp rats", "chinks", "gooks", "nips" or "zipperheads". Be aware that these expressions are highly offensive and that Walt is **not** a good role model in this respect!

2. "Reading" a movie

"When we experience a film, we consciously prime [meaning: "prepare"] ourselves for illusion. Putting aside will and intellect, we make way for it in our imagination. The sequence of pictures plays directly on our feelings. Music works in the same fashion; I would say that there is no art form that has so much in common with film as music. Both affect our emotions directly, not via the intellect."

Ingmar Bergman, Swedish director (1918–2007) (one of the most accomplished filmmakers ever)

When we watch a film in a movie theater, it is exactly this experience that we are looking for. When the lights are turned off and noises die down, we let ourselves be drawn into the film, we get totally absorbed by the story; the feelings of the protagonists invade our bodies: We are scared to death, we are moved to tears, we are sick at heart. For about two hours the film seems to take control of our consciousness and rule over our imagination. It is this manipulative power that makes films so attractive to us as consumers. However, the questions of why and how films are so powerful can add a fascinating new dimension to the film experience. Instead of just watching the movie and getting lost in its world, we can "read" the movie as a carefully designed piece of art and discover the cinematic techniques that influence our expectations and emotions. Moreover, as already mentioned at the beginning of this introduction, we can also understand a movie as a mirror of the culture(s) in which it was created and which it represents.

Here are some different levels of understanding a movie:

Level of understanding	Task	Questions
Understanding **the plot**	Describe	**What** is the setting? **What** are the people saying? **What** is happening/ **What** happened before? **What** is the atmosphere?
Understanding the **cinematic techniques**	Analyze	**How** is the story told? **How** is the mood created? **What cinematic devices** are used to express characters' feelings or thoughts?
Understanding the movie as a **product of its culture**	Interpret	**What beliefs, values, cultural concepts** are mirrored in the movie?

3. Independent research

If you get "hooked" by the movie, you might be interested in doing some research on your own.
Here are some suggestions:

- Clint Eastwood the actor, director and producer
- Film locations of *Gran Torino*
- The city of Detroit
- The Hmong people
- Clint Eastwood the politician
- Eastwood's latest movies: *American Sniper* (2014), *Sully* (2016)

III. Gran Torino

1. Gran Torino: Synopsis of the plot

Setting: Detroit, state of Michigan, USA. Walt Kowalski's house is in Highland Park, a neighborhood in the north of the former 'Motor City'.

Chapter/ running time	Summary	Quotes
Chapter 1 00:00:00 – 00:03:43	[Opening credits/theme tune *Gran Torino*] Dorothy Kowalski's funeral At his wife's funeral Walt Kowalski shows contempt for both the shallow sermon of Father Janovich, and his own sons and grandchildren, who behave in a disrespectful and self-absorbed way.	"Don't you think he'll get in trouble by himself in the old neighborhood?" "He's still living in the 50s."
2 00:03:44 – 00:08:22	**Walt's family and neighbors** At the funeral reception at his house, Walt can hardly bear the people around him: His grandsons sneak around in his basement and find a box full of mementos from Walt's time as soldier in the Korean War, among them a Silver Star medal. Meanwhile his Asian neighbors are having a party with many guests. Walt's teenage granddaughter Ashley discovers his immaculate Gran Torino in his garage and wonders if she could inherit it. The shy Hmong teenager from next door, Thao Van Lor, disturbs the reception asking if he can borrow a starter cable and is rudely sent away. The priest asks Walt to come to confession, because Dorothy had wanted it. Walt outspokenly refuses to do so.	"How many swamp rats can you get in one room?"
3 00:08:23 – 00:12:39	**Thao and his family** The Hmong guests are arriving when Walt's guests are leaving. The family is celebrating the birth of a baby with traditional rituals. Thao has problems fitting in. Father Janovich makes another attempt to approach Walt and is kicked out once again.	"How can he ever become the man of the house?"
4 00:12:40 – 00:17:21	**Thao's initiation** Thao is bullied by members of a Hispanic gang driving by in a car. Thao's older cousin Spider and his friends see this happening and chase them away. In return they expect Thao to join their gang. Thao refuses at first but is finally willing to undergo an initiation test: stealing Walt's prized car, a 1972 Gran Torino Sport.	"Is you a girl or is you a boy, man? I can't tell."
5 00:17:22 – 00:20:03	**Locals at the bar** Walt is telling racist jokes in a bar when the persistent Father Janovich shows up and talks Walt into chatting about life and death. They have a beer and Walt actually opens up and shares some of his haunting memories of the battlefields in Korea.	"Sounds like you know a lot more about death than you do living!"
6 00:20:04 – 00:23:19	**Thao's crime [theme tune 'Gran Torino'].** Late at night, Walt thwarts Thao's attempt to steal the Gran Torino. The boy only gets away because Walt falls and hurts himself. The next day Walt's son Mitch calls, pretending to ask only how his father is, the real reason is he wants season tickets for football. In the evening, Walt polishes his immaculate Gran Torino in the driveway before proudly admiring it from his porch.	"Ain't she sweet."
7 00:23:20 – 00:27:36	**Walt saves Thao** At night Spider and his gang show up at Thao's house and try to force him to get in their car with them. Sue stands up to them verbally, but the conflict quickly turns into a violent fight between Thao's family and the gang. Then Walt suddenly shows up and chases the intruders away with his rifle – the same weapon with which he had shot a teenage boy in the Korean War. The next day Walt finds his porch full of presents. The Hmong see him as community hero because he saved Thao. Sue introduces her family, undaunted by Walt's insolent behavior. Thao apologizes for trying to steal the Gran Torino but Walt only warns him to never set foot on his property again.	"Get off my lawn."

Chapter/ running time	Summary	Quotes
8 00:27:37 – 00:30:21	**Walt and the priest** Hearing about the fight the night before, Father Janovich visits Walt. He is upset that Walt didn't call the police. He begs him to go to confession, saying it will release him from past burdens. Walt does not want to go, but shows more respect for the priest.	"The thing that haunts a man most is what he isn't ordered to do."
9 00:30:22 – 00:34:47	**Walt saves Sue** Sue and her white date Trey get into trouble with three black teenagers on the sidewalk. They start sexually harassing Sue, who courageously defends herself verbally. Walt happens to pass by in his car and intervenes after observing the scene. The gang only let Sue go after Walt pulls his pistol. Walt sends Trey off and gives Sue a ride home.	"These guys don't want to be your bro and I don't blame them."
10 00:34:48 – 00:38:33	**Sue and Walt in the truck** In the truck Sue explains to Walt who the Hmong are and why Thao appears to be so weak. Later, while reading the newspaper on his porch, Walt is positively surprised when he observes how Thao helps an elderly lady with her grocery bags.	"He [Thao] just doesn't know which direction to go in."
11 00:38:34 – 00:41:56	**Walt's birthday** Mitch and his wife Karen visit Walt on his birthday – as it turns out only to try to persuade him to leave the house and live in a senior's retirement home. They get kicked out. Walt celebrates his birthday alone on his porch. Sue shows up as he has just emptied his last beer can and convinces him to join the Hmong barbecue next door.	– "Just keep your hands off my dog." – "No worries. We only eat cats."
12 00:41:57 – 00:46:42	**The Hmong party** Walt feels uncomfortable among the Hmong until Sue introduces him to their code of behavior and he gets to enjoy their delicious food. Walt is disturbed when the Hmong shaman "reads him", accurately analyzing his life in only a few sentences. Sue is truly worried about Walt when she sees him coughing blood.	"I have more in common with these gooks than I do (with) my own rotten family."
13 00:46:43 – 00:51:41	**Walt's lecture** Finally Walt enjoys being surrounded by the Hmong ladies flattering and spoiling him with lots of food. Then Sue takes him downstairs to the basement, where the young Hmong are hanging out. Thao is sitting unhappily in a corner of the room. Walt rudely tells him off for not asking Youa, a good looking Hmong girl who is apparently interested in Thao, for a date.	"I never thought you were worse with women than you are at stealing cars."
14 00:51:42 – 00:54:42	**Thao's amends** Thao's family insists on Thao making up for trying to steal the Gran Torino. He is to work for Walt to pay his debt. On the first day, Walt makes Thao count the birds in the tree.	"You just go over there and count the birds."
15 00:54:43 – 00:58:33	**Thao's formation** From the second day on, Walt really sets Thao to work. He makes him fix the dilapidated house across the street. Thao works very hard all week, cleaning up the neighborhood [theme tune: 'Gran Torino']. Walt's coughing gets worse.	"You want me to watch paint dry?"
16 00:58:34 – 01:01:41	**Walt's diagnosis** Walt is irritated because he is no longer to be treated by his (presumably) white male doctor, Dr. Feldman, but by a young female Asian, Dr. Chu. Walt calls his son Mitch to tell him about his fatal diagnosis. Mitch, however, is so self-absorbed that he doesn't realize what his father is telling him [theme tune: 'Gran Torino']. From his porch, Walt observes how Spider and the gang still don't leave Thao alone.	"This kid doesn't have a chance."

Chapter/ running time	Summary	Quotes
17 01:01:42 – 01:07:47	**Mutual support** Thao asks Walt to help him fix a faucet in the kitchen. When Walt sees that Thao really would like to fix their rundown house he gives him some tools. In his garage Walt finds out that Thao only tried to steal the Gran Torino because he had been under pressure from the Hmong gang. Thao is concerned when he witnesses Walt coughing up blood. Then Walt asks for Thao's help to carry a freezer up the stairs from the basement. Sue comments on the irony that Walt lets Thao wash the car he had tried to steal from him and thanks him for looking after her brother, who doesn't have a father.	Sue: "He [Thao] doesn't have any real role models in his life."
18 01:07:48 – 01:13:18	**Manning up Thao** While Thao is working in Walt's garden they talk about Walt's life – his job as an assembly worker for Ford, his army service, his son's job, his illness – and about Thao's future. Walt offers to "man Thao up", get him a job and a date with Youa. He sees manliness at the barber shop: Walt and his friend try to teach him "how real men talk".	"Of course I have to make a little adjustment and man you up a little bit."
19 01:13:19 – 01:16:46	**Thao's job** Walt uses his connections to get Thao a job at a construction site, where Thao can prove that he has learned the language of real men. At a hardware store they buy a tool belt and some basics for Thao's new job. Thao thanks Walt for his support.	"What do you wanna do? Carry your tools in a rice bag?"
20 01:16:47 – 01:19:29	**The assault** On his way home, Thao is attacked by his cousin's gang. He bravely tries to defend himself but has no chance against five men. He tries to hide the assault as some of Walt's tools got broken. When Walt finds out a few days later, he wants revenge.	"Cowards!"
21 01:19:30 – 01:22:40	**Walt's revenge** Walt drives up to the gang's house and beats up Smokey, second in command in the gang, threatens him with a gun, warning him to leave Thao alone. Next day Walt has Thao, Sue, their mother and Youa over for a BBQ in his backyard. When he finds out that Thao has asked Youa out on a date, he asks him if he wants to take the Gran Torino.	"If I have to come back here, it's gonna get fucking ugly."
22 01:22:41 – 01:25:34	**The gang's retaliation** While Walt is watching TV at home one night, the Hmong gang drives by and shoots up Thao's home with machine guns. Walt goes over. Thao has been injured slightly, but Sue is missing. Sitting at the table waiting for Sue, Walt questions his act of vendetta. When Sue finally turns up, raped and badly beaten, Walt is devastated and leaves.	"In the war, we just lost a lot of friends, but you're kind of set for it."
23 01:25:35 – 01:29:38	**Walt's reaction** In the darkness of his house, Walt blames himself. He smashes the glass doors of his kitchen cabinet with his knuckles. Father Janovich comes in to find out what Walt is going to do. Drinking a can of beer in the darkness of the room, they talk openly. It becomes clear that Walt feels he has to destroy the gang.	"You know, Thao and Sue are never gonna find peace in this world."
24 01:29:39 – 01:32:33	**Walt's preparations** In the morning, Thao enters Walt's house, agitated. He demands immediate action but Walt manages to calm him down and make him wait until the afternoon. Walt mows his lawn, takes a bath, gets a hair cut and a straight shave at the barber's and buys a fitted suit, something he has never done in his life.	"Now is the time to stay calm."

Chapter/ running time	Summary	Quotes
25 01:32:34 – 01:34:37	**Walt's confession** Dressed up in his new suit, Walt goes to see Father Janovich. When Walt says he wants to make a confession, the priest fears that he has killed someone or plans to do so. It turns out that Walt's worst sin was that he was never close to his sons. The priest absolves him of his sin and tries to find out his plan, urging him to not seek vengeance.	The Father and Walt "Go in peace." "Oh, I am at peace."
26 01:34:38 – 01:39:29	**Walt gearing up** Walt is cleaning his rifle in the kitchen when Thao shows up at the appointed time. Thao is eager to kill the gang although he has never used a weapon in his life. Walt takes Thao to his basement to give him his Silver Star, a medal he earned in Korea, where Walt killed at least 13 people. Then he locks Thao up in the basement to take revenge alone. He confesses to killing an innocent, teenage soldier. Walt wants to prevent Thao from carrying such a haunting burden, too. Walt calls Thao his friend. Thao is outraged as Walt leaves. Father Janovic and the two police officers who have been watching Smokie's house for hours get orders to leave. Father Janovic had obviously alerted the police that Walt might show up seeking retribution. Sue finally hears Thao's shouting and sets him free. He runs to drive to Smokie's house, Sue follows him.	"I got blood on my soul. I'm soiled."
27 01:39:30 – 01:41:46	**Walt's ruse** Walt is standing still in front of Smokie's house. He is patiently waiting until the Hmong thugs notice him through the half-open blinds and step out onto the porch. Walt condemns them for their crime: raping a girl from their own family. Alerted by the noise, many neighbors witness the scene. The "miniature cowboys", as Walt calls them, pull their guns when Walt gets a cigarette out of his outer jacket pocket. With his hand he gestures to shoot them, his index finger pointing at each one of them. Then he reaches slowly into his inside jacket pocket – it looks like he is about to pull a gun. He is immediately brutally executed by deafening bursts of automatic gunfire. He falls backwards onto the ground and lies there, his arms spread like Jesus on the Cross. His right hand opens to reveal not a gun, but his 1st Division Cavalry Zippo lighter, covered in blood.	"Me I've got a light"
28 01:41:47 – 01:46:29	**Justice** [theme tune: 'Gran Torino'] Walt is lying on the ground, almost peacefully, when the police show up. When Thao and Sue arrive in the Gran Torino, a Hmong officer tells them what happened, and that the gang will now be put in jail for a long time. Thao, Sue (her face still terribly bruised) and Father Janovich watch Walt being carried into a vehicle and the gang members being led away by the police. Probably a few days later, Thao, Sue and their mother leave their house in traditional Hmong clothes to go to Walt's funeral. In church, Walt's family is looking skeptically at the Hmong people across the aisle. Father Janovich's sermon reveals his close relationship to Walt and his deep admiration for him. Later Walt's family and Thao sit together at the lawyer's office where Walt's will is being read out. To the family's surprise and disappointment, the house goes to the Church and the Gran Torino to his friend Thao [theme tune: 'Gran Torino']. This scene fades into Thao driving his new car with Daisy the dog by his side.	"These guys will be locked up for a long time."
29 01:46:30–51:47	Thao is driving along the shore of Lake Saint Claire. [credits]	"Gentle now a tender breeze blows"

2. The Ambiguity of Belonging: an overview

The Hmong people:
Geo-political ambiguity of belonging
The Hmong are an ethnic group from the hilly regions of China, Thailand, Vietnam and Laos. In the second half of the 20th century, the US Army recruited Hmong men from Laos to fight against the communists during the cold war. As a result, several hundred thousand Hmong people fled from Laos to Thailand as political refugees. Thousands of Hmong migrated to the West, mostly the US.

Thao:
Social and cultural ambiguity of belonging
Thao is a second generation Hmong American, born in the US. He is a hybrid character, caught between Hmong and American cultures. His mother is more traditional, insisting on the Hmong way of life. He cannot identify with his cousin's Hmong gang. His father is absent, but described as "old school". This gap is filled by Walt, who teaches Thao aspects of the American way of life (working, how to communicate, dating, relying on oneself, etc).

Personal ambiguity of belonging:
Family, groups, career, gender
Thao doesn't seem to fit in anywhere. He can't meet his family's expectations as the "man of the house" and refuses to join the Hmong gang. Before Walt helps him to "man up", he has no job. He is teased for his feminine looks and not being a "real man". The jobs he does are stereotypically seen as "women's work" – doing the dishes or gardening. Thao is usually a girl's name. He is an outsider with no close relationships – only Sue seems to understand him.

Walt:
Social and cultural ambiguity of belonging
Walt no longer fits into "the old neighbourhood", where he lives. He is one of the few white people left in a part of Detroit, which, in better days, used to be white and middle-class. His house sticks out among the run-down ones of his Hmong neighbors. He is like a fossil: the last survivor of an older generation of "real Americans" with "decent", conservative values. This is symbolized by the immaculate, deeply treasured Gran Torino in his garage. Also by his white Ford truck, which he drives around town, "saving the Helpless from the Wicked".

Personal ambiguity of belonging:
Family, religion
Walt feels alienated from his own family. His two sons moved out with their families to a wealthy suburb (Grosse Point Park). They appear self-centered, greedy, disrespectful and superficial. Despite his racist attitudes towards his neighbors, he feels more closely connected to the traditional Hmong culture than to his "own" 21st century, decayed American one. The relationship to Thao and Sue becomes much closer and more caring than the one to his own sons has ever been. Walt shows his contempt for the church as an institution, but he develops a close relationship to Father Janovich. Walt feels burdened and alienated from himself. He did things in the past that do not match his personal beliefs and values: he killed people, even teenagers, in the war and feels he hasn't been a good father.

IV. Worksheets

Film terminology: How to analyse a film

Here are some illustrations of the most important film terminology for use in your discussions.

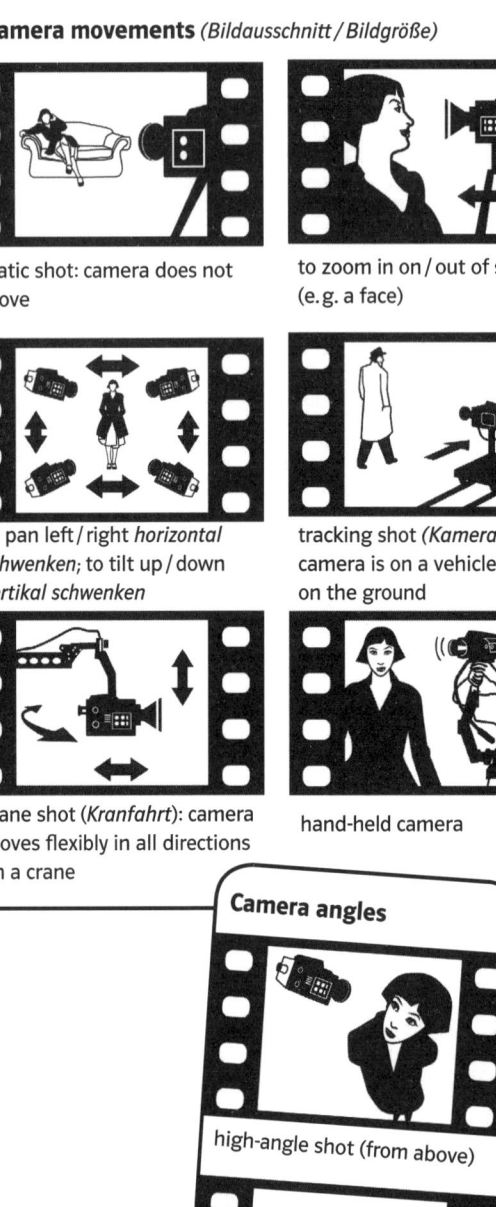

Camera movements *(Bildausschnitt / Bildgröße)*

static shot: camera does not move

to zoom in on / out of sth. (e.g. a face)

to pan left / right *horizontal schwenken*; to tilt up / down *vertikal schwenken*

tracking shot *(Kamerafahrt)*: camera is on a vehicle moving on the ground

crane shot *(Kranfahrt)*: camera moves flexibly in all directions on a crane

hand-held camera

Field size
(Bildausschnitt / Bildgröße)

long shot *(Totale)*; people / objects shown from a distance

full shot: shot of the whole body / object

medium shot: upper body / part of an object

close-up *(Nahaufnahme)*: head and shoulders

extreme close-up: *(Detailaufnahme)* face only; detailed shot

Camera angles

high-angle shot (from above)

eyelevel shot

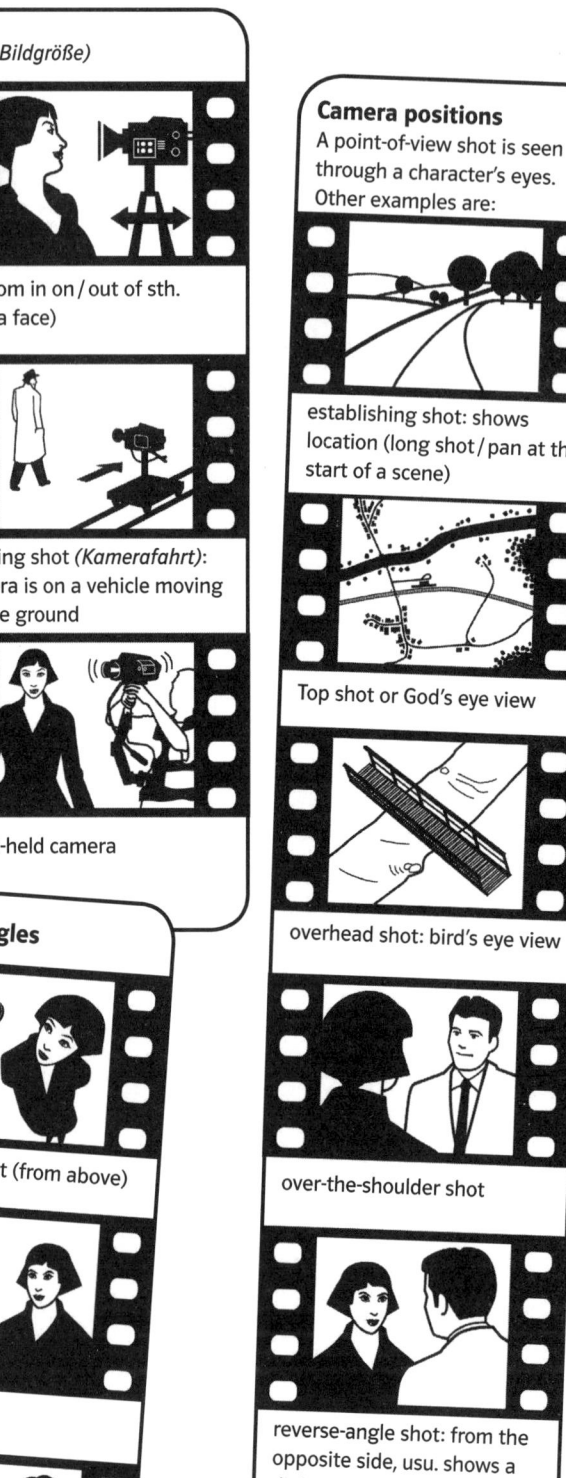

Camera positions

A point-of-view shot is seen through a character's eyes. Other examples are:

establishing shot: shows location (long shot / pan at the start of a scene)

Top shot or God's eye view

overhead shot: bird's eye view

over-the-shoulder shot

reverse-angle shot: from the opposite side, usu. shows a dialogue partner

Gran Torino: Movie trailer

1. *Read through the adjectives in the box and make sure that you understand what they mean. They are all taken from film reviews of Gran Torino. Copy them into the table, sorting them into positive, neutral and negative adjectives. Add more adjectives which can be used to describe and evaluate a film and sort them.*

realistic – vigorous (forceful, dynamic) – predictable – touching – humorous – insightful – macho –
gritty (unsentimental, harsh) – clichéd – entertaining – well-paced (with a good speed) –
earnest (serious, intense) – thought-provoking – radical – compelling (convincing, fascinating)

Positive	Neutral	Negative

2. *Watch the trailer and choose three to five adjectives that you consider to be most OR least suitable to describe the movie, judging from the trailer. Discuss your choice with your partner.*

3. *The trailer reveals conflicts between different characters or groups of characters. Watch the trailer again and use arrows to indicate where you think conflicts exist in the character web. Highlight the conflicts you expect to be most dominant in the movie.*

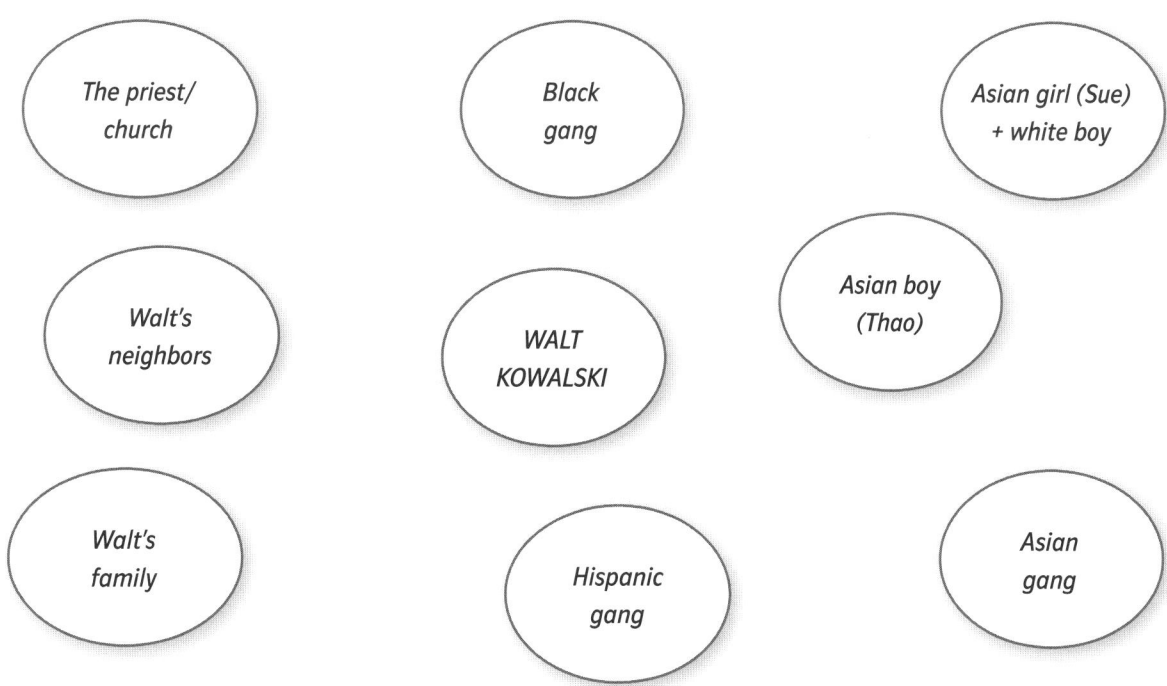

Gran Torino: Movie poster

1. *Look closely at the poster and make a rough sketch of the picture in the box below. Focus on lines, shapes and contrasts. Interpret your findings and discuss them with your neighbor. The expressions below might help.*

> *a horizontal / vertical / straight / diagonal line*
> *There is a clear / well-defined / straight line that runs from ... to ...*
> *The most dominant lines in the foreground ...*
> *The shape of the lines reminds me of ... / resembles ...*
> *There is a(n) obvious/ remarkable / sharp contrast between ... and ...*
> *X and Y form/ express a stark / striking / strong contrast, which could stand for ...*
> *The contrast might mirror ... / could be interpreted as ...*

2. *Write down anything you associate with the movie poster right into your sketch.*

3. *With your partner, speculate about the movie's possible genre, storyline (plot) and themes.*

Gran Torino: Speed viewing

1. *Universal themes are general ideas about the human condition. They deal with human concerns that are not influenced or caused by cultural differences or where we live. They raise questions about the relationship of human beings to themselves, to each other and to the universe. Make sure you know the meaning of all the themes in the list. Mark the ones that personally concern you now. Share your thoughts about one or two of them with your neighbour if you feel comfortable with this.*

abundance/scarcity	*freedom*	*peer pressure*
abuse of power	*friendship*	*perseverance*
action vs. apathy	*greed*	*prejudice*
authority	*guilt and innocence*	*pride*
beauty	*heritage*	*quest for knowledge*
coming of age	*heroes*	*religion*
courage	*honesty*	*repentance*
effects of the past	*justice*	*revenge*
faith	*love and hate*	*security/safety*
family	*loyalty*	*seizing the moment*
fate	*need for change*	*survival*
fear	*obligation*	*the road not taken*
fear of failure	*parent-child relationships*	*war and peace*

2. *Watch the first half of the movie in the 16X fast forward mode. From the list of universal themes choose at least five you think play a major role in the movie. Justify and discuss your choice with your neighbor.*

3. *Even though Clint Eastwood's movie deals with universal themes, it is clearly a product of its culture. Watch the first half of the movie again – this time in the 16X rewind mode – and note down moments or images you consider to be typically American. Explain what ideas you connect with these "American moments" or icons and what they stand for. Discuss if they relate to any of the universal themes in particular.*

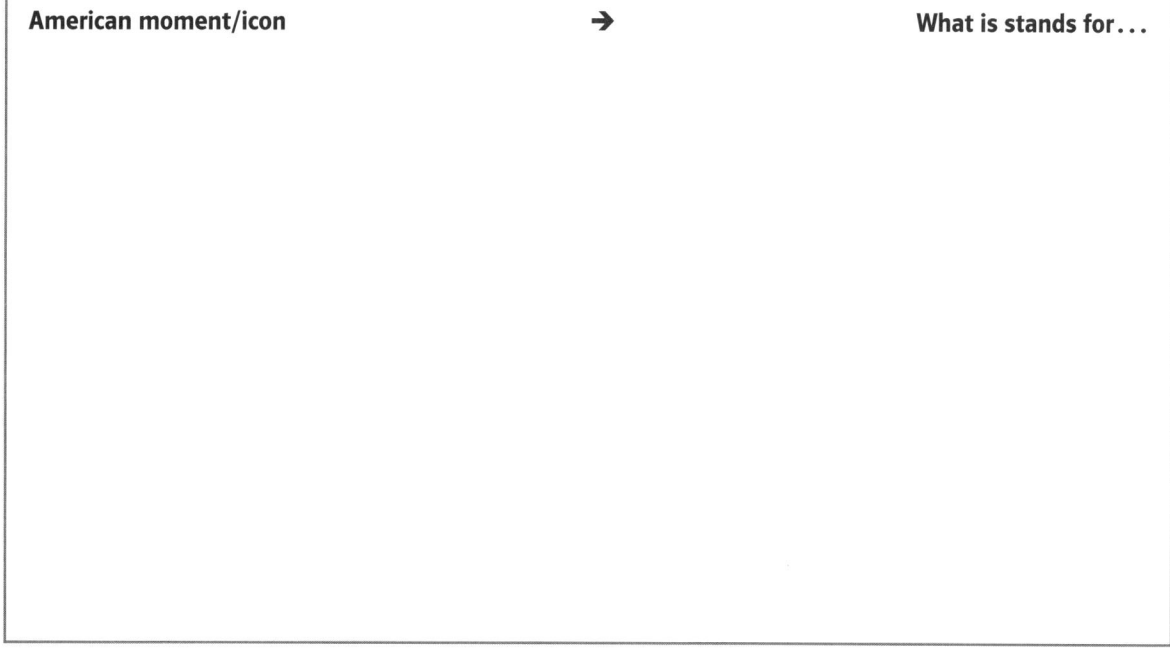

American moment/icon	→	**What is stands for...**

4. *The speed viewing doesn't really help us understand the title of the movie. Think of an alternative title that captures themes and symbols you see as central to the film. Discuss your ideas with your neighbor.*

Historical background

1. *Read the text and be prepared to explain the context of the photo and the map below to your partner (highlight relevant passages, take notes).*

2. *Once you have exchanged your information find connections between the two texts.*

The Korean War (1950–1953)

US Corsair fighter planes over a US warship during
the Korean War. Sept 4 1951.

World War II divided Korea into a Communist northern half and an American-occupied southern half, divided at the 38th parallel. The Korean War (1950–1953) began when the North Korean Communist army crossed the 38th Parallel and invaded non-Communist South Korea. As the North Korean army, armed with Soviet tanks, quickly overran South Korea, the United States came to South Korea's aid. General Douglas MacArthur, who had been overseeing the post-WWII occupation of Japan, commanded the US forces, which now began to hold off the North Koreans at Busan, at the southernmost tip of Korea. Although Korea was not strategically essential to the United States, the political environment of the Cold War at this stage was such that policymakers did not want to appear "soft on Communism." Officially, the US intervened as part of a "police action" run by a UN (United Nations) international peace-keeping force; in actuality, the UN was simply being manipulated by US and NATO anti-Communist interests.

In 1953, a peace treaty was signed at Panmunjom that ended the Korean War, returning Korea to a divided status which was essentially the same as before the war. Furthermore, neither the war nor its outcome did much to lessen the era's Cold War tension.

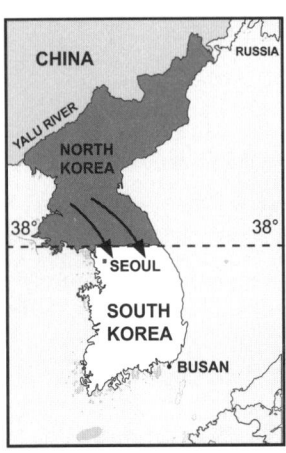

June 25, 1950

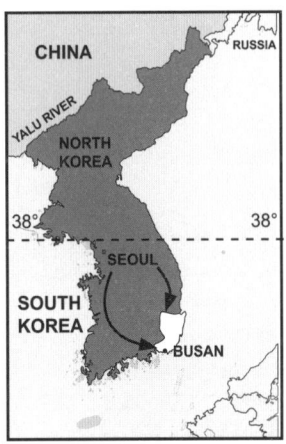

Sept. 14, 1950

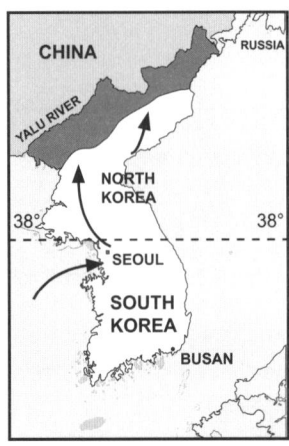

Nov. 25, 1950

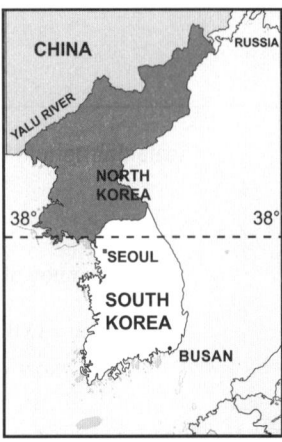

July 27, 1953

Historical background

1. *Read the text and be prepared to explain the link between the photo and the map below to your partner (highlight relevant passages, take notes).*
2. *Once you have exchanged your information find connections between the two texts.*

The Hmong and the "Secret War" (1964–1973)

Vietnam Veteran's Memorial in Washington DC.

The Secret War began around the time the US became officially involved in the Vietnam War. In the early 1960s, the US Central Intelligence Agency (CIA) began to recruit, train and lead the indigenous Hmong people in Laos to join fighting the Vietnam War. The Hmong ([mãŋ]), are an Asian ethnic group from the mountainous regions of China, Vietnam, Laos, and Thailand. About 60 % of all Hmong men in Laos joined the "Secret War". Hmong soldiers put their lives at risk in the front line, fighting for the US to block the <u>supply line</u> and to rescue downed American pilots. From 1967–1971, 3,772 Hmong soldiers were killed in the war, 5,426 injured or disabled.

Following the US withdrawal from Vietnam in 1975, the Lao kingdom was overthrown by the communists and the Hmong people became targets of <u>retaliation</u> and persecution. While some Hmong people returned to their villages and attempted to resume life under the new regime, thousands more fled to Thailand, often under attack. This marked the beginning of a mass exodus of Hmong people from Laos. Those who did make it to Thailand generally were held in <u>squalid</u> United Nations refugee camps.

Many Hmong refugees were resettled in the United States after the Vietnam War. Beginning in December 1975, the first of them arrived in the U.S., mainly from refugee camps in Thailand; however, only 3,466 were granted asylum. In May 1976, another 11,000 were allowed to enter the United States, and by 1978 some 30,000 Hmong people had immigrated. It was not until the passage of the Refugee Act of 1980 that families were able to enter the US, becoming the second wave of Hmong immigrants. Today, about 210,000 Hmong people reside in the United States. The majority of these live in three federal states: California (ca 66,000), Minnesota (46,000) and Wisconsin (32,000).

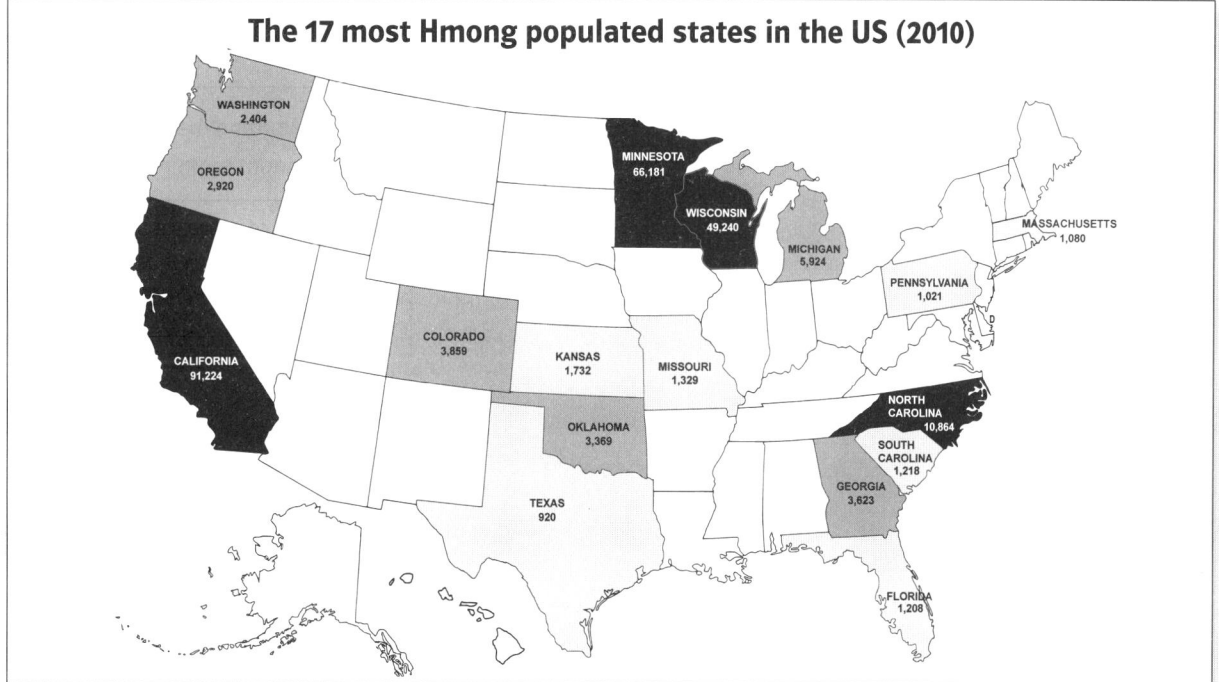

The 17 most Hmong populated states in the US (2010)

8 **supply line** – *Versorgungszufuhr*; 12 **retaliation** – revenge; 15 **squalid** – dirty, neglected

Detroit – the two-sided city

In 1903 Henry Ford founded the Ford Motor Company in Detroit, establishing the city's status as the world's automotive capital – "Motor City". With the expansion of the automobile industry in the early 20th century, Detroit became the fourth largest city in the country. Industrial restructuring and loss of jobs in the auto industry led to a considerable loss in population from the late 20th century to the present
5 *– from a peak population of 1.8 million in 1950 to less than 714,000 in 2011. In 2013, the city of Detroit declared a financial emergency and filed for bankruptcy, which was successfully exited in 2014.*

For the past two years, I have taken postgraduate students in urban geography to Detroit, where
10 a prosperous downtown is rising. The city's transformation is being celebrated and seen as a potential model for other places.

But George Galster, professor of urban studies at Detroit's Wayne State University told my
15 students to imagine the city as a bathtub. The new investments and activities are like water pouring into the tub. But nothing has been done to plug the giant hole at the bottom of the tub. This new renaissance does not address why Detroit
20 declined in the first place. It does little to address poverty, unemployment and access to resources

Detroit, 2015. The Renaissance Center in downtown (left).

for the vast majority of the city's residents. What's worse, the <u>gentrification</u> of downtown Detroit contributes to greater inequality and polarisation, which are growing challenges for cities around the world. What has created this hole at the bottom of the bathtub?
25 Between 2000 and 2010, 25 % of the population left the city – that's an average of 2,000 people a month. Half of its 5–9 year olds departed during this time, their parents leaving in search of better schools and opportunities in the suburbs. Today, Motor City boasts just two vehicle assembly plants, down from more than two dozen at its peak. Neighbourhoods which used to house factory workers look like rural prairie. This exodus of jobs has led to a mismatch of people and employment across
30 the region. Around 60 % of Detroiters who have a job work in the suburbs. Conversely, 70 % of the jobs located in the city of Detroit go to people who live in the suburbs. Chronic unemployment and poverty remain one of the city's biggest challenges.

The current renaissance does not address these problems. Most investment takes place in the Greater Downtown, which includes the city's historic core and neighbourhoods such as Midtown and
35 Corktown, which comprise 5 % of the city's area and population. Here, once-abandoned offices are being bought up and renovated by enthusiastic entrepreneurs, a new modern tram line is being built along Woodward Avenue and it can actually be difficult to find an apartment as vacancy rates are very low. The boundaries between revival and decay can be very severe. Travel three minutes by car from Midtown's Wayne State University and you are surrounded by streets overgrown by vegetation and
40 burned out factories.

Greater Downtown's current revival will mean that this 5 % of the city will pull further and further ahead of the other 95 %. Those able to afford to live there enjoy great restaurants and bars, well-paid employment, safe and attractive neighbourhoods and reliable public transit. The problem is most Detroiters cannot afford to live here. And like everything else in Southeast Michigan, race is one of the

22 **gentrification** when middle-class people move into (and take over) neighbourhoods where poor people live

45 dominant factors. In a city that is 85 % African American, Greater Downtown is becoming increasingly white.

There are also growing divides between public and private services. While most Detroiters wait hours for the police to arrive, private security forces patrol Downtown and around Wayne State University. When problems arise in adjacent neighbourhoods, you don't call 911, you call campus
50 police, who respond in minutes, rather than hours. New public transport investments are increasingly focusing on Detroit's core. There is a sad irony that in a city where about a quarter of residents are too poor to own a car, the new tram line will serve office workers and students in Greater Downtown. It will do nothing for the low-income families that need to travel 15 km by bus to access a basic grocery store. So while there is indeed a "renaissance" taking place in Detroit, most city residents are detached
55 from it.

This inequality is part and parcel of contemporary cities. It is not confined to cities struggling with the legacy of de-industrialisation; polarisation is also one of the biggest challenges facing prosperous cities such as London, New York or Paris. But inequality doesn't just happen. It is the product of economic, business and political decisions of what, how and where to invest and distribute money
60 and resources.

Brian Doucet, in *The Guardian*, 17 February 2015

Read the text and tick the correct statement as indicated. Use a quotation from the text to support your decision. Give the line number(s) plus the first three and the last three words of the quotation. If the quotation is less than six words, write down the full quotation. EXTRA: Speculate on connections between the text and the movie.

1. The bathtub metaphor tries to illustrate

☐ that downtown Detroit has become a prosperous, comfortable place.
☐ that the development of the city serves as a model for other cities.
☐ that recent investments have little effect on the poor.
☐ that recent investments have finally plugged up the hole in the bathtub.

Line(s) … _____

2. In the past 15 years Detroit has changed because

☐ many car plants were moved to the suburbs.
☐ many families fled to the suburbs.
☐ neighbourhoods where workers used to live have become gentrified.
☐ most jobs are located in the Greater Downtown.

Line(s) … _____

3. Midtown and Corktown are neighbourhoods

☐ where you can only live if you have a decent income.
☐ that haven't profited from the recent revival.
☐ where whites are a minority.
☐ where you depend on a car.

Line(s) … _____

Task sheets for theme group: Prejudice and racism

1. Getting started: Everyday racism

What language do you speak in Korea? Asian?

a. *Discuss what this real life situation reveals about the speaker's mindset. Share examples of everyday racism that you have experienced or witnessed and discuss what options you have to react to overtly racist remarks or jokes.*

"The less secure a man is, the more likely he is to have extreme prejudice."
"People have lost their sense of humor. In former times, we constantly made jokes about different races."

b. *In your group discuss the meaning and validity of Clint Eastwood's above remarks on racism.*

2. Watching the movie: Walt Kowalski's racism

a. *Racism is about more than words. Take notes to describe how Walt Kowalski expresses his racism.*

LANGUAGE	BEHAVIOR/ACTIONS
What he says and how he says it:	*How he behaves towards the Hmong:*

b. *Examine if Walt's racism undergoes a development in the course of the movie. Visualize your findings graphically or in a drawing. Compare your findings in your group and agree on one visualization.*

c. *Discuss if Walt is a through and through racist, a racist at heart, or if his racism is only a manly façade.*

3. Watching closely: Roots of racism

a. *After rescuing Sue from the black gang. Walt talks to her for the first time in his truck. Closely watch chapter 10 again (DVD 00:34:48 – 00:38:33/YouTube: Gran Torino (clip 6 – part 2) "Where the hell is Humong, I mean Hmong, anyway?"). Analyze what Walt thinks about the Hmong and how Sue reacts.*

Walt's preconception about the Hmong	Sue's reactions

b. *"Racism is rooted in ignorance". Discuss this statement in reference to the scene. Find other reasons for Walt's racism.*

c. *At the beginning of the scene, Sue is the victim who is rescued by Walt. In the course of the conversation, however, Sue proves that she can easily keep up with Walt. Analyze the cinematic techniques that are used to emphasize that Walt and Sue are on the same level.*

Camera angle	Field size

→ Although Walt is clearly taller and physically stronger than Sue, the way the camera presents them emphasizes that…

4. Exploring further: Eastwood accused of racism

a. *Gran Torino has definitely raised people's awareness for the history and culture of the Hmong minority in the US, but there are also many critical voices. Read the text, highlight the accusations against Eastwood and come up with counter-arguments.*

Though many of the people who have seen the film may have gotten a sense of satisfaction and joy from seeing that Walt overcame his racism, the people who acted as the Hmong members in the movie did not. They were offended by the traces of racism that were included in the movie and that they experienced themselves on set.

5 Vang, who played Thao in the film, said he and the other Hmong actors were treated unfairly. Eastwood would not allow them to tweak their lines (even though he claimed that he did allow them to when asked in interviews following the release of the movie) [...].

The actors felt degraded when they were told to "make noise" by rambling words in their language. The Hmong actors were also left out by their fellow cast members who were white.

10 The cast members excluded them from cast events because they immediately assumed that Hmong actors were exactly like their character counterparts—unable to speak English clearly or to understand anything "American."

Vang also mentioned that he was upset by the way the Hmongs were portrayed in the film. He did not want the Hmong community—his own community—to be seen in a negative light by the

15 audience. He pointed out that tea ceremonies were not performed correctly, that some of their important political lines in the script were not subtitled into English, and that these inaccuracies led to misconceptions of the community. [...]

The movie itself contained many racial slurs about Asians that the speakers found insulting. In the scene in which Walt takes Thao to his friend's barber shop, Thao is called names such as

20 "pussy kid," "dick smoking Guk head" and "chink." These degrading words imply that Asians are feminine and homosexual.

From: thebottomline.as.ucsb.edu

b. *In your group act out a round table with Clint Eastwood, Nick Schenk (spreenplay writer), Bee Vang (Thao Van Lor) and Ahney Her (Sue Lor). Take roles. Discuss whether Gran Torino is a movie about racism or a racist movie.*

Notes

Task sheets for theme group: Masculinity

1. Getting started: The man card

A "man card" doesn't really exist. It is an imaginary "certificate" which shows that a man is a "respectable" member of the male community and has proven that he is "a real man". Example: "We had to take away Henry's man card because he cried in public when Kristina dumped him". (urbandictionary.com)

In your group discuss what tasks you could add to a (stereo)typical "man card". Then think about your own ideas of manliness: What requirements does a man (not) have to meet to be a real man in your eyes?

EXTRA: Design a "lady card".

2. Watching the movie: Walt's masculinity

a. *Describe and analyze different aspects of Walt's masculinity throughout the film: What makes him a 'real man'? The grid below might help you to structure your findings.*

Actions/Deeds	Language	Symbols (actual objects)

b. *In your group, discuss which manly attributes you consider to be undesirable, although they are part of Walt Kowalski's positive image as tough guy and savior of the weak.*

3. Watching closely: Manning up Thao

a. *Walt teaches Thao how to speak and act like a man. Compare Thao's manliness before and after the lesson at the barber's. Closely watch chapter 18 (DVD 01:07:48 – 01:13:18/YouTube: Gran Torino (clip 11) "What do you want to do with your life, kid?") and 19 (DVD 01:13:19 – 01:16:46/YouTube: Gran Torino (clip 13) "He knows construction") again. Analyze how Thao's development is supported by the camera.*

	In the backyard	At the construction site
Content: the setting and Thao's actions (what image does this give him?)		
Language: how Thao speaks and reacts		
Camera angle		
Field size		
Conclusion		

b. *Compare your results in the group. Discuss Walt's role for Thao: teacher, friend, father? Something else?*

4. Exploring further: Femininity in Gran Torino

The movie revolves around two male protagonists, some critics have called it macho. Do you agree?

Sue is perhaps the only rounded character. From 1 to 10, how do you rate Sue's strength (1 = very weak, 10 extremely strong)? In your group compare your assessment and justify your point of view.

Is Sue a hero or a victim? Discuss her role in the film.

Task sheets for theme group: Gran Torino

1. Getting started: The significance of cars

"Cars are an extension of our personality. Cars really are another layer of clothing. Owning a car is like a rite of passage for most men."
"Men love cars because the better their cars look, the more manly they feel."
[Leslie Kendall, curator of Peterson Automotive Museum, Los Angeles]
"Most men love cars because the better their cars look, the more manly they feel." [Ahney Whitney Her, the actress who plays Sue in the movie]

The distinctive form of the Gran Torino Sport

a. *In your group discuss what these statements mean and if you personally agree. What role do cars play in your life and the life of your family and friends?*

b. *The Gran Torino (Sport) was a special version of the Ford Torino, an automobile which was produced in Detroit for the North American market between 1968 and 1976. The car was named after the city of Turin (Torino, in Italian), which was seen as "the Italian Detroit". The Gran Torino (Sport) was first produced in Detroit in 1972.*

Describe the car. Who do you expect to sit behind the wheel of such a car? Speculate about what role this car might play in the movie and why its name was chosen as the title of the movie.

2. Watching the movie: The role of Walt's Gran Torino

a. *Describe and analyze at least three scenes in which the Gran Torino plays a role. Use the table below.*

Action	Significance for Walt or Thao	EXTRA: Function of the scene for the movie
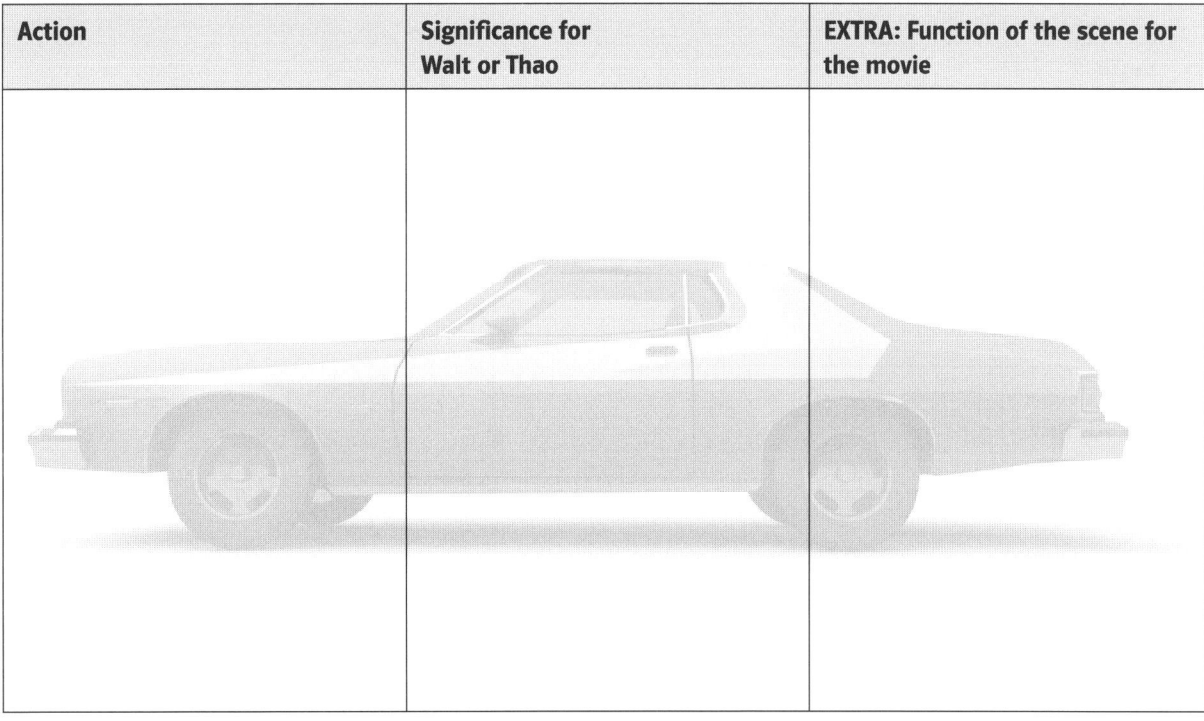		

b. *"It's the Gran Torino that brings Walt and Thao together."*
   In your group compare your results and discuss if you agree with this statement.

3. Watching closely: Looking after the Gran Torino

a. *Closely watch two short scenes again: Walt polishing his Gran Torino (DVD 00:22:28 – 00:23:19/YouTube: "Gran Torino, clip 4: Your number one son") and Thao inheriting the Gran Torino and driving away on Lake Shore Road (DVD: 01:45:26 – 01:46:29/"Gran Torino ending scene"). Describe and analyze Walt's relationship to his car in the first scene and its role as Walt's legacy in the second, final scene. Analyze the cinematic techniques that emphasize Walt's/Thao's emotions and their effect.*

	Scene 1: Walt and his Gran Torino	Scene 2: Thao inheriting Walt's legacy
Emotions		
Camera: (angle and field size)		
Colors/lighting		
Music (theme song: *Gran Torino*)		
Role/ significance of the Gran Torino		

b. *"The car is just a symbol of part of Walt. Walt sort of is the Gran Torino."*
   In your group compare and discuss your results and relate them to this quote by Clint Eastwood.

4. Exploring further: Movie cars

In your group make a list of movies where a car or other vehicle plays an important role. Discuss the function of the car for the movie. Does the car have a "personality"? Does it influence the plot in ways the characters do?

[TIP: The "Internet Movie Cars Database" has a good list of motor vehicles.]

That **Aston Martin**

_____

_____

_____

_____

_____

_____

_____

_____

_____

Task sheets for theme group: Violence

1. Getting started: Violence starts with thoughts

> *"Nonviolence means avoiding not only external physical violence but also internal violence of spirit."*
> Martin Luther King Jr.

a. *In your group, explain the meaning of this quote. Describe the development of violent conflicts you know from your own experience, from the news or from literature and films.*

b. *Make a graph or chart which shows how a conflict ending in death might develop. You can use the pyramid and the phrases given. Work on your own, then compare the different versions within your group.*

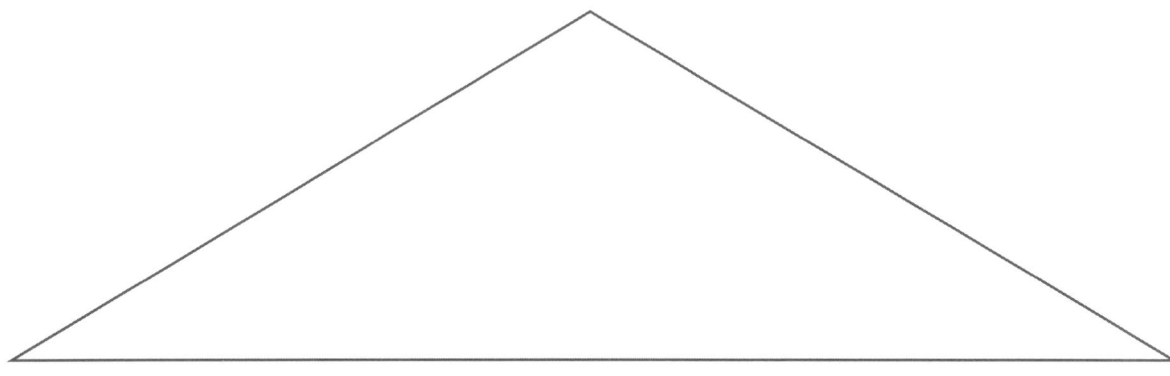

intimidating – armed assault – pushing physically – attacking verbally – teasing / ridiculing sb's appearance or behavior – threatening – committing murder / suicide – standing in sb's way – ignoring and excluding sb – spreading rumours – physical assaults – harassment by groups – shoot out

2. Watching the movie: Escalating violence

a. *While watching, note down scenes that lead directly to or show increased violence. Use your results from task 1 to comment on the level of violence that is reached in each scene. Compare findings in the group.*

Characters involved	Violent behavior	Your comment

b. *Discuss what Walt could have done to prevent the conflict from escalating.*

3. Watching closely: Walt as a hero of violence

a. *Re-watch the first part of chapter 7 (DVD: 00:23:20 – 00:25:46/YouTube: Gran Torino (clip 5 – part 1) "Get off my lawn"). Analyze the film techniques used to create atmosphere. Compare your findings in your group (word bank below!). Discuss other techniques that could have been used to create suspense.*

Action	Atmosphere	Film techniques (camera movements, lighting, sounds/music)
The Hmong gang show up at the Van Lor's house and verbally put pressure on Thao to join their gang.		
Gang members violently force Thao to get into their car.		
Walt shows up and chases the intruders away, threatening them verbally and with his rifle.		

Word bank: tense, aggressive, turbulent, playful, gloomy (dark), cold, hostile, terrifying, threatening, merciless, alarming, chaotic, panicky, nervous, worried, lively, ambivalent, frantic, frightening, out of control

b. *In your group discuss the validity of the following statements (at least two).*
   "The 'Get-off-my-lawn' scene ...
   - ... is an urban version of a typical western."
   - ... illustrates the US American belief in self-reliance and self-defense."
   - ... turns Walt Kowalski into a hero of violence for the neighborhood."
   - ... is one of the funniest scenes in the movie."
   - ... is an example for the usefulness of the "Castle Law", which permits a homeowner to use deadly force to defend himself or herself against an intruder.

4. Exploring further: Representation of violence in films

Films are often mirrors of the culture that produces them. Discuss if and why Gran Torino can be seen as an expression of American concepts, beliefs and values – especially as related to the topic of violence.
Discuss what a German version of Gran Torino might look like.

Task sheets for theme group: Religion

1. Getting started: existential questions and religious symbols

a. *Explain the meaning of these two symbols (a candle and a cross) in Christianity. What role might they play in the movie?*

b. *In your group, think of existential questions that play a role in religion(s), e.g. "What is the meaning of life?" Discuss what questions and themes you expect to encounter in Gran Torino.*

_____

_____

_____

2. Watching the movie: References to the Christian faith

a. *Clint Eastwood's film is full of open and hidden references to the Christian religion. Note down the elements of Christianity that are shown in the movie (in chronological order). Summarize your findings for your group. Compare your results and discuss their significance.*

Phrase of film	Elements of Christianity
Beginning	*1ˢᵗ official confession in church* *2ⁿᵈ personal confession to Thao*
Ending	

b. *"Me I have got a light". Discuss the symbolism of light and the Christian cross (crucifix) in the movie.*

3. Watching closely: Walt's death

a. Closely watch chapter 27 (DVD: 01:39:30 – 01:41:46/YouTube: "Gran Torino Walt Kowalski death scene") and describe the religious allusion in it. (Hint: stop the film when Walt is lying on the ground. Who does he resemble?) Analyze the film techniques used in Walt's final appearance and interpret their effect on the viewer. Focus on color and lighting, camera angle, field size and camera movement.

	Description	Effect
Colors and lighting		
Camera angle		
Camera movement		
Field size		

b. "Walt sacrifices himself to make up (atone) for his sins." Analyze this statement and discuss these sins.

c. Walt does not act according to conventional Christian wisdom – represented by Father Janovich – which teaches repentance ("confession") in Church followed by forgiveness for your sins. In your group discuss the two positions: Should you personally make up for your sins by (if you can) repairing what you have destroyed, or should your sins just be forgiven through Jesus the Savior, after a confession? Are there any other ways of repenting your faults and sins, in your opinion?

4. Exploring further: Invisible religion

"Films and other media function as "invisible religion", says sociologist Thomas Luckmann. Just like traditional religions, they raise existential questions like: 'What is the meaning of life?', 'Is there a life after death?', 'How can we find forgiveness?' and 'What is good, what is evil?' And they offer answers to those questions to provide guidance and to make sense of our existence."

Discuss this theory, referring to other movies.

Excel in language: Prejudice and racism

1. *Complete the grid by matching the given paraphrases with the words or phrases in the box below.*

race riot – racist (noun) – racist (adjective) – race relations – racism – racial profiling – racial	

1.	way of behaving or thinking that shows you don't like or respect people from other races, and that you believe your race is better than any other one
2.	someone who does not like or respect people from other races, and who believes their race is better than any other one
3.	relating to racism (*rassistisch*)
4.	relating to race (*Rassen-*)
5.	the relationships between people of different races who live in the same community
6.	an occasion when people of different races who live in the same community fight violently against each other
7.	the practice of thinking that people of a particular race or colour will behave in a particular way, especially in a criminal way

2. *Add the missing prepositions.*

a. to discriminate _____ someone   (*jemanden benachteiligen*)

b. to feel discriminated _____ by someone   (*sich durch jemanden benachteiligt fühlen*)

c. to have prejudices _____ someone   (*Vorurteile haben gegenüber jemandem*)

d. to feel superior _____ someone   (*sich jemandem gegenüber überlegen fühlen*)

e. to feel inferior _____ someone   (*sich jemandem gegenüber unterlegen fühlen*)

Excel in language: Masculinity

1. *The words in the box are adjectives that are commonly – which does not necessarily mean suitably (!) – used to describe either femininity or masculinity. Make sure you understand what they mean before categorizing them into the grid. Add more adjectives if you can.*

dependent, emotional, ambitious, aggressive, rebellious, accepting, submissive, self-confident, graceful, flirtatious, active, forceful, protective, individualistic, non-emotional, nurturing, tough-skinned, self-critical, competitive, passive, independent, sensitive, athletic, understanding, tender, dominant, vulnerable

Adjectives commonly associated with <u>masculinity</u>	Adjectives commonly associated with <u>femininity</u>

2. *Match the verb on the left to the collocations to get a list which describes (stereo)typical male behavior. Some verbs match more than one noun phrase.*

to rise (rose, risen) – to offer – to take (took, taken) – to provide – to adopt – to demonstrate – to suppress – to use	sb protection (*jdm. Schutz gewähren*) – violence against sb (*Gewalt gegen jdn. anwenden*) – one's emotions (*seine Gefühle unterdrücken*) – to a challenge (*eine Herausforderung annehmen*) – safety to sb (*jdm. Sicherheit gewähren*) – revenge on sb (*sich an jdm. rächen*) – the father role for sb (*für jdn. die Vaterrolle annehmen*) – one's strength (*seine Stärke zeigen*)

1. to rise to a challenge

2. _____

3. _____

4. _____

5. _____

6. _____

7. _____

8. _____

9. _____

10. _____

11. _____

12. _____

Excel in language: Gran Torino

1. *The following expressions are all taken from the movie. Write down their German equivalents. Add at least two more car expressions to the list. Use a dictionary to find the correct English translations.*

1. a vintage car	
2. a stunning/gorgeous/shiny car	
3. to be in mint/perfect condition	
4. to get into a car	
5. to slam the door	
6. to drive off in a car	
7. to screech the tires	
8. a vehicle pulls up to a place	
9. to hook a jumper cable to a dead battery	

2. *The verb 'to drive' (drove, driven) can have different meanings. Match the sentences with meanings.*

1. Do you promise to drive carefully?	*To force someone to leave a place.*
2. Stop driving yourself so hard.	*To make someone extremely angry.*
3. She drove him to the airport.	*To control a vehicle (as a driver) carefully.*
4. You're driving me up the wall.	*To make someone work or try very hard.*
5. They were driven out of their village.	*To take someone to a place in a vehicle.*

3. *A 'drive' is not necessarily a ride in a car. Find the other meanings of this noun in these sentences:*

a. *16500 Mulholland Drive, Los Angeles, CA* _____

b. *Insert the DVD into your disk drive.* _____

c. *She worked all weekend. She's full of drive and ambition.* _____

_____

d. *He didn't act rationally. He is totally controlled by his desires and drives.* _____

_____

Excel in language: Violence

Carefully go through these lists of collocations, looking up ones whose meaning or pronunciation you do not know for sure (e.g. www.macmillandictionary.com). Highlight and write in the table below the ones you think will be most helpful when talking about violence in Gran Torino.

ADJECTIVE + *VIOLENCE* – *Example: considerable violence* – considerable, great, excessive, extreme, large-scale, serious, continuing, escalating, growing, unnecessary, mindless, random, uncontrolled, brutal, criminal, unlawful, institutionalized, widespread, sporadic, domestic, physical, sexual, drug-related, communal, ethnic, racial, political, revolutionary, terrorist, left-wing, right-wing

VERB + *VIOLENCE* – *Example: engage in a conflict* – engage in, inflict violence on sb, resort to, turn to, suffer, provoke, denounce, deplore, hate, reject, breed (Hatred breeds violence), to quell the violence, be capable of (We're all capable of violence sometimes).

VIOLENCE + VERB – *Example: Violence broke out.* – break out, erupt, occur, escalate into, intensify, worsen, spread

VIOLENCE + PREPOSITION – against (violence against police officers), among (violence among football supporters), between (violence between rival ethnic groups), towards (violence towards ethnic minorities), within (violence within the family)

PHRASES – (punish) an act of violence, (call for) an end to violence, (be prepared for) an eruption/outbreak of violence, fear of violence, (live) a life of violence, (be prone to) outbursts of violence, a (downward) spiral of violence, a threat of violence, a victim of violence, a refuge for victims of domestic violence, violence breeds more violence, a wave of violence

Word / collocation	Meaning/pronunciation

Excel in language: Religion

This word bank might help you to talk about the movie and its religious themes.

> to deliver a eulogy – *eine Grabrede halten* • to repent/to show remorse for sth – *Reue zeigen* • to make atonement/to atone for a sin – *Sühne leisten für eine Sünde* • Christ crucified – *der gekreuzigte Christus*

The following expressions are all taken from the movie. Write down their German equivalents. Think of at least three more useful expressions related to religion. Use a dictionary to find English translations.

1. to go to confession	
2. to confess one's sins to sb/a priest	
3. to admit one's guilt	
4. to make amends	
5. to leave one's burden behind	
6. to absolve a person of his/her sins	
7. to reach one's salvation	
8. He would roll over in his grave if he saw that.	
9. the Our Father/Lord's Prayer	
10. "In the name of the Father, the Son and the Holy Spirit"	
11. to preach about life and death	
12. a (church) service	

Theme group: Presentation

As a group prepare a presentation in which you share the results with the others. Summarize and visualize the main points on a poster or with a presentation program (PowerPoint, Keynote). You have 15–20 minutes to:

- Name your topic and comment briefly on it.

- Introduce about five to seven new words and phrases that you consider necessary or useful to talk about your topic. Write them onto the poster or a slide before the presentation so that you don't lose too much time. Make sure you know how to pronounce the words correctly (an online dictionary is the easiest way to find out, e.g. www.macmillandictionary.com, www.merriam-webster.com).

- Summarize the significance and context of your theme within the movie.

- When/how/how often does it occur? What message does it convey? What function does it have? What effects does it have on the viewer? What questions does it raise? What cinematic devices are used to draw the viewer's attention to it?

- Show one film scene (maximum: five minutes) or two shorter scenes (max. three minutes each) to illustrate your results. You can choose a scene you have worked on in your tasks or you can look for another scene and apply your insights to this new sequence.

Make sure that you split the speaking time evenly in your group.
Be well prepared so that you can speak freely and don't have to ask for words.

After your presentation your classmates will be able to ask questions. Your teacher might bring up questions and issues that you have discussed in your theme group.

Useful general words and phrases for presenting (and their meanings)

1. Starting your presentation "Today we're going to look at …"
2. The main points "Firstly: …; Secondly: … Next let's look at …"
3. Concluding "Finally, …" "In conclusion, …"

Theme groups: Wrapping up

While the other theme groups are presenting their results, work on the following tasks:

1. *Copy the words and phrases of each group into the table.*

2. *Gran Torino is a movie that deals with the big questions of American life. Use the theme web to note down these big questions as they are mirrored in the movie. Include insights from your own group work.*

3. *Find connections between the different themes. Visualize and verbalize them in the theme web.*

English word/phrase	Paraphrase/German translation

Gran Torino: Theme Web

Racism

Masculinity

Violence

Gran Torino

Religion

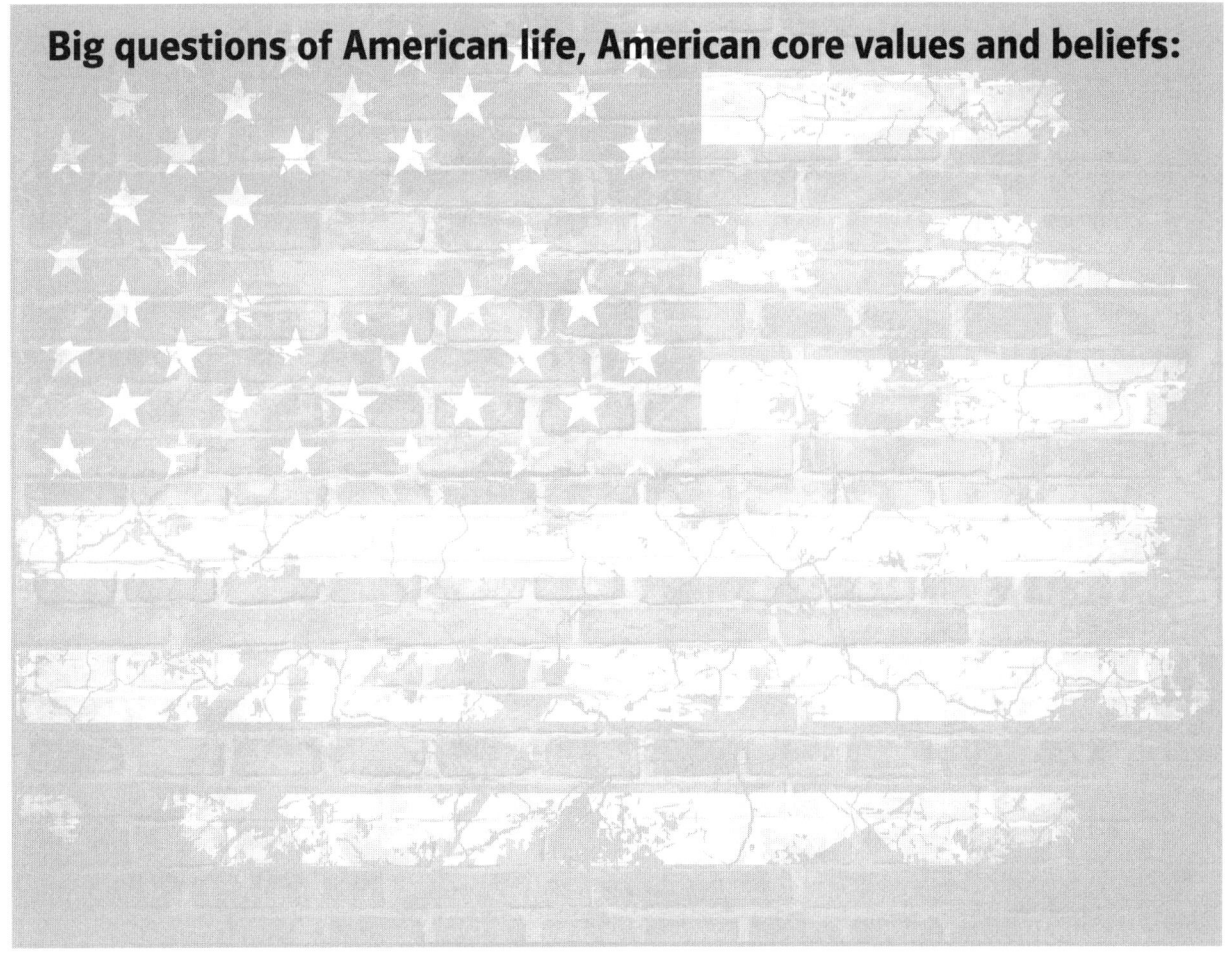

Big questions of American life, American core values and beliefs:

Introduction: Identity and belonging (text A)

a. *Get together with a partner. You each have a different text. When you have finished reading, explain the graphic below to your partner, based on the information you have read. As you read, note phrases you can use.*

b. *After your presentations, summarize together how the two texts are related.*

Your identity defines who you are. Your sense of identity and belonging is influenced by numerous factors, including your experiences, relationships and your environment. Finding your identity and belonging can be hard since we are challenged by the questions who we are, who the others want us to be and where we belong. No one can answer these questions for us. It is our personal view that

5 influences our decisions. Identity is multifaceted since your identity is shaped by a combination of different traits. You do not only possess one specific identity but may change your own identity depending on the environment and the people that surround you. For example, you may be extrovert with your family but rather reserved and serious with your school friends. You may speak a different language (e.g. different vocabulary and intonation) with your parents than with you soccer team. We

10 adjust our identity in order to fulfil our desire to belong.

Here are some facets of our identity:

personal: personality traits, qualities, skills, appearance, gender; **family:** role in the family; **career:** profession; **social:** social class, community, peer group, co-workers, clubs, gang; **ethnic/religious:** race, traditions, language, religion; **national:** origin and place of residence, language; **cultural:** ethnicity,

15 religion, history

Everything and everyone can influence a person's identity and belonging. For different people, the same experience may affect them completely differently. Although we all live in the same world where many of our experiences overlap, the reason why we are all unique is because we ultimately choose what does or does not impact us in a crucial or unimportant way.

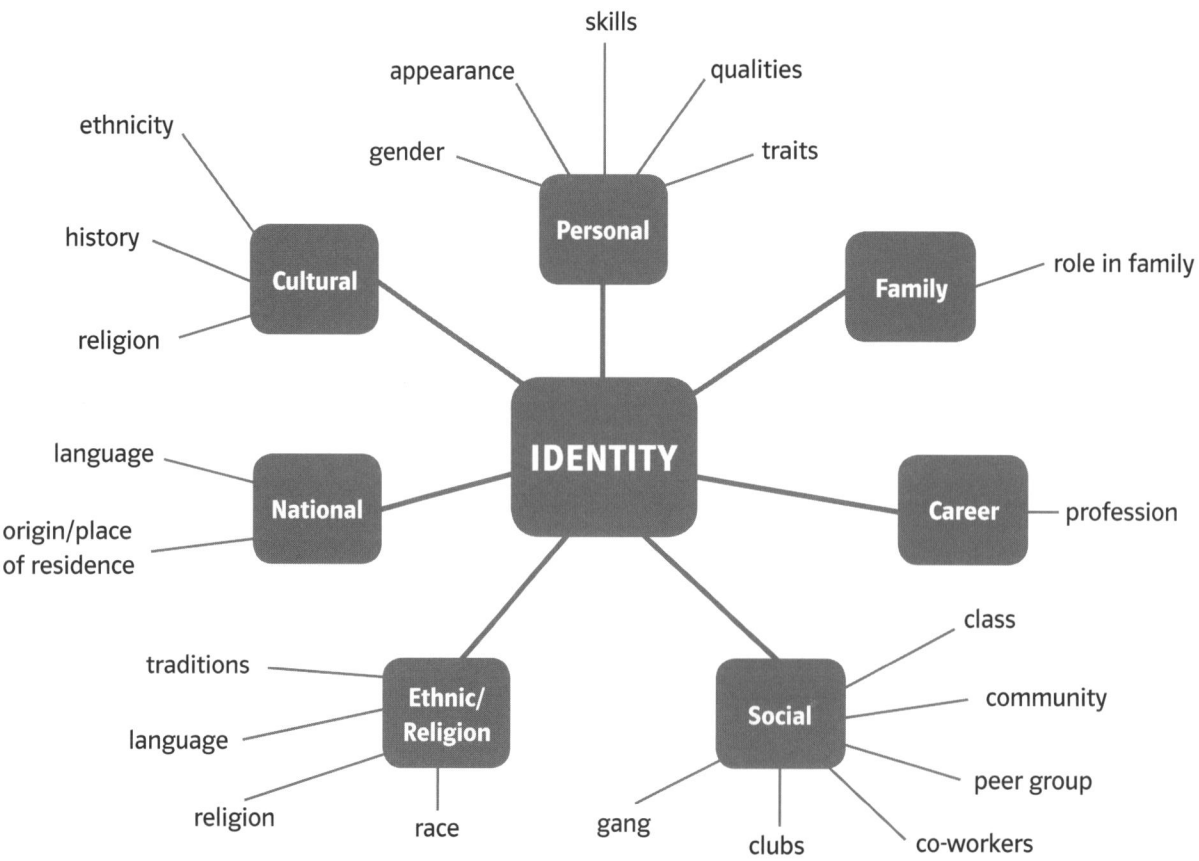

Introduction: Belonging as basic need (text B)

a. *Get together with a partner. You each have a different text. When you have finished reading, explain the graphic below to your partner, based on the information you have read. As you read, note phrases you can use.*

b. *After your presentations, summarize together how the two texts are related.*

Abraham Maslow (1908–1970) was an American psychologist best known for his 'hierarchy of needs', a psychological theory centered on our inborn desire for fulfillment. His levels of basic needs are often represented in a pyramid. The theory states that a person does not feel the second need until the demands of the first have been met, nor the third until the second is met, and so on. Here are Maslow's needs:

5 **1. Physiological Needs**
These are biological needs for oxygen, food, water and warmth. They are the strongest needs because they come first in a person's search for satisfaction.

2. Safety Needs
With all physiological needs satisfied, those for security become active in unstable times or emergency.

10 **3. Needs for Love, Affection and Belongingness**
The next class that emerges consist of the needs for love, affection and belongingness. There are many different forms of belonging: relationships (e.g. family, friends, partners, pets), social groups (e.g. classes, clubs, gangs, church, co-workers, organisations, communities) and environments (e.g. nation, race, region, city, culture). Many people become susceptible to loneliness or even depression if they lack a sense of belonging.

15 **4. Needs for Esteem**
When the first three classes of needs are satisfied, the needs for esteem can become dominant. These involve needs for both self-esteem and for the esteem a person gets from others. Humans have a need for a stable, high level of self-respect, and respect from others. When these needs are satisfied, the person feels self-confident and valuable as a person in the world. When these needs are frustrated, the person feels inferior, weak, helpless 20 and worthless.

5. Needs for Self-Actualization
When all of the foregoing needs are satisfied, then and only then are the needs for self-actualization activated. Maslow describes self-actualization as a person's need to be and do that which the person was "born to do." "A musician must make music, an artist must paint, and a poet must write."

The Ambiguity of Belonging: Quotes

> *"I don't even remember the season. I just remember walking between them and feeling for the first time that I belonged somewhere."*
> **Stephen Chbosky, in: The Perks of Being a Wallflower**

a. *Make a sketch of the image the quote evokes for you. Who are "I" and "they"? What might be the reason for the speaker's feeling of belonging? Compare your results with your neighbor(s).*

b. *Reflect on your own experiences: When do you have the feeling that you belong (to a person, to a group, to a community, to a nation), and why? Share your thoughts with your partner.*

c. *Read the quotes below and mark the ones that appeal to you most. Discuss your choice with your partner.*

> *"You can search high and low to find happiness on earth, yet unless you love yourself, you will never find your true belonging."*
> **Leon Brown, author**

> *"A sense of belonging is not physical. We can't find it by changing where we live or what we do. We have to carry it within us."*
> **Phyllis C. Cast, author**

> *"Happiness, I think, has to come in the beginning, truly, from feeling a sense of well-being within yourself. To me it's that incredible sense of belonging and peace within your own self and heart that really is joy."*
> **Goldie Hawn, actress and film producer**

> *"We know that where community exists it confers upon its members identity, a sense of belonging, and a measure of security. ... Communities are the ground-level generators and preservers of values and ethical systems".*
> **John Gardner, author**

> *"A deep sense of love and belonging is an irreducible need of all people. We are biologically, cognitively, physically, and spiritually wired to love, to be loved, and to belong. When those needs are not met, we don't function as we were meant to. We break. We fall apart. We numb. We ache. We hurt others. We get sick."*
> **Brené Brown, author**

> *"The dynamism of any diverse community depends not only on the diversity itself but on promoting a sense of belonging among those who formerly would have been considered and felt themselves outsiders."*
> **Sonia Sotomayor, Associate Justice of the Supreme Court of the US**

The Ambiguity of Belonging: Ethnic minorities

1. Pre-viewing: Belonging to Germany

What defines a person's "Germanness"? Rank the criteria, indicating which are the most important and least important to you. Add more if you want. Compare and discuss your result with your neighbour.

- The person was born in Germany.
- The person lives in Germany permanently.
- The person works and pays taxes in Germany.
- German is the person's mother tongue.
- The person's outer appearance does not reveal that (s)he belongs to a different ethnic group.
- The person has assimilated to German traditions and habits.

2. While-viewing: Prejudices

a. *Watch the video clip "What kind of Asian are you?" Outline both the man's assumptions about the woman and the <u>actual</u> facts.*

The man's assumptions about the woman	Actual facts about the woman

b. *Explain what the clip criticizes in a humorous way.*

3. Post-viewing: The ambiguity of belonging

a. *Assess how realistic/exaggerated the video clip is. What effect do such everyday experiences have on the sense of belonging of ethnic minorities (e.g. Asian-Americans, African-Americans, Latino-Americans) in the US?*

b. *Discuss if and how you could make a similar video about Germany. Write a dialogue for such a clip. Be prepared to act it out for the class or to make a short film.*

The Ambiguity of Belonging: Language of belonging

1. *Look at the German meanings of the two single words 'ambiguity' and 'belonging'. Come up with some idiomatic translations for the phrase 'the ambiguity of belonging'. It does not have to be a word by word translation.*

Ambiguity: **Belonging:** Zugehörigkeit

Ambiguität
Ambivalenz
Doppelbödigkeit
Doppeldeutigkeit
Doppelsinn
Doppelsinnigkeit
Mangelnde Eindeutigkeit
Mehrdeutigkeit
Unbestimmtheit
Uneindeutigkeit
Unklarheit
Vieldeutigkeitkeit
Zweideutigkeit

The Ambiguity of Belonging: **Translations**

2.

"There is a reason why the word 'belonging' has a synonym for 'want' at its center; it is the human condition."
Jodi Picoult

Solve the riddle: What is the center of the word 'belonging' which is a synonym for 'want'?
Look the word up in a good collocation dictionary and find prepositions, adjectives and verbs that go with the word.

3. *In the list of 18 words, find eight synonyms for 'ambiguity' and eight for 'belonging'. Two words do not fit in.*

incertitude – kinship – vagueness – affinity – double meaning – transition – uncertainty – attachment – loyalty – relationship – doubtfulness – challenge – enigma – obscurity – inclusion – unclearness – acceptance – association

Ambiguity ~ _____

_____

_____

_____

Belonging ~ _____

_____

_____

_____

4. *Complete the grid by writing the German translation into the right-hand column. Add at least two more verbs that are useful to talk about the idea of belonging or not belonging. Write at least five sentences about the characters in Gran Torino using different verbs from the list.*

Verb + complement	Examples	Translation
to belong (somewhere)	*Please put the books where they belong! / This is the place I belong.*	
to belong to somebody	*Who does this car belong to?*	
to belong to something	*She belongs to the local film club.*	
to belong to somebody/ something	*He belongs to Mr. Bennet's group, not mine.*	
to feel a sense/have a feeling of belonging	*At church, I finally felt a strong sense of belonging.*	
to join sth	*He joined the chess club in 2015.*	
to join sb for sth	*Would you like to join us for dinner?*	
to identify with sth	*He can't identify with their beliefs.*	
to participate in sth	*She agreed to participate in the meeting.*	
to take part in sth	*They refused to take part in the discussion.*	
to be/feel part of sth	*Joe felt like part of the family.*	
to exclude sb from sth	*They excluded him from the meeting.*	
to be/feel excluded from sth/sb	*She felt excluded from the agreement.*	

Sentences:

a. _____

b. _____

c. _____

d. _____

e. _____

5. *Go through these words and phrases. Write down those not yet in your active vocabulary. Use a dictionary!*

share everything with sb – long to belong – do the right thing – have friends –
be part of a community – trust in sb – have confidence in – happiness – rely on sb –
feel respected by sb – be free to be oneself – form a team – be different but the same –
(not) be judged – group acceptance – feel connected – be a part of sth – join a group –
give/receive hugs – have a place to go (to) – everyone is different – hope – care for sb –
be at ease – feel comfortable/secure/safe/included – group member – organization – club –
association – similar – alike – control – be suitable – fit in – ethnicity – boundaries – be related to –
a strong/close bond – establish a connection with – play together – work together – laughter –
one of a kind – be accepted for who you are – stand out – have sb on your side –
mutual understanding – togetherness – support each other – assist each other –
have sympathy for sb – show undivided loyalty to sb – partnership – feel included/excluded –
be close to sb – feel responsible for sb – look after sb – be committed to sb – sacrifice oneself for sb –
share (the) responsibility for sth

The Ambiguity of Belonging: Character development

1. Walt's belongingness

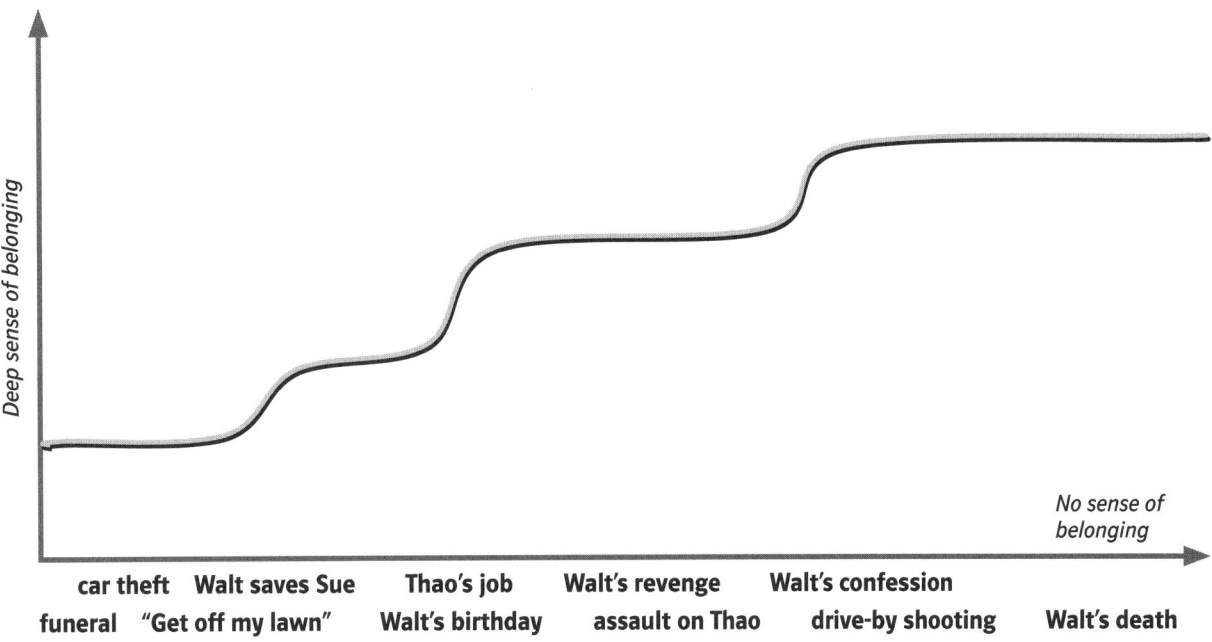

Deep sense of belonging

No sense of belonging

| car theft | Walt saves Sue | Thao's job | Walt's revenge | Walt's confession | |
| funeral | "Get off my lawn" | Walt's birthday | assault on Thao | drive-by shooting | Walt's death |

The line illustrates how Walt's sense of belonging towards Sue changes in the course of the movie. Use different colors to show: Walt's feeling of belonging towards: his sons (red); Thao (blue); and the priest (green). Compare and discuss results with your neighbor. Assess what the diagram tells you about Walt Kowalski.

2. Thao's belongingness

Draw a diagram for Thao, illustrating his sense of belonging towards Sue, his family and Walt. Compare and discuss results with your neighbor. Assess what the diagram tells you about Thao.

Deep sense of belonging

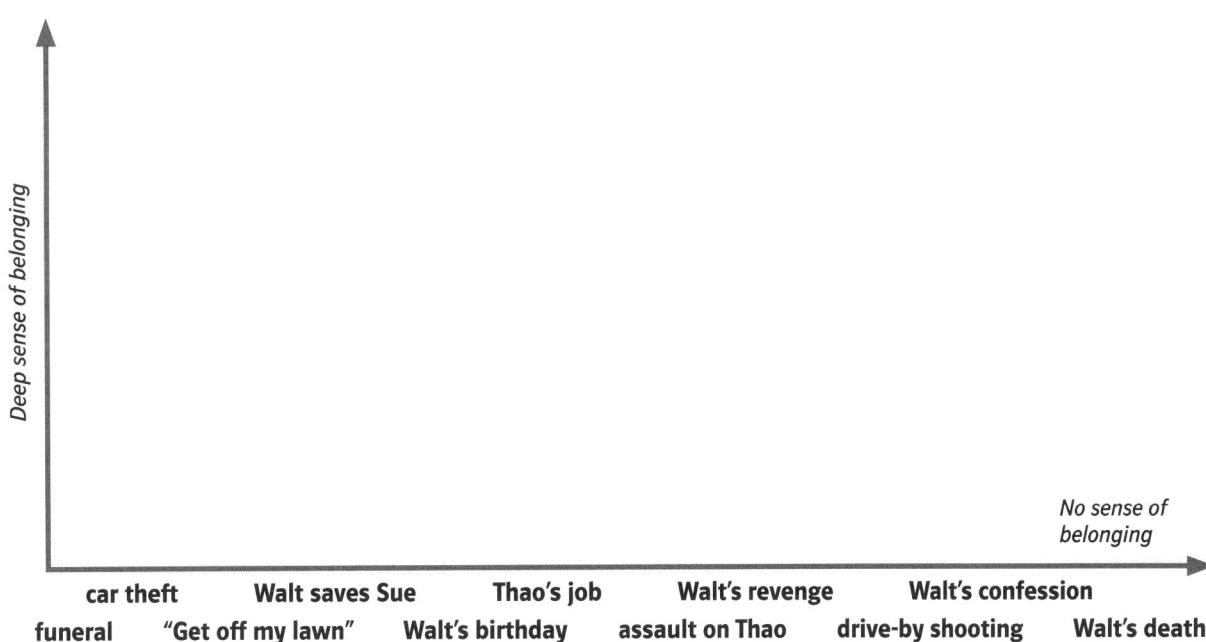

Deep sense of belonging

No sense of belonging

| car theft | Walt saves Sue | Thao's job | Walt's revenge | Walt's confession | |
| funeral | "Get off my lawn" | Walt's birthday | assault on Thao | drive-by shooting | Walt's death |

The Ambiguity of Belonging: Opening sequence (00:00:00 – 00:12:39)

1. Chunk box

> **to attend a funeral service** to take part in a religious ceremony when sb has died – **to deliver/give a eulogy** to give a speech at a funeral about the person who has died – **to act in a disrespectful, impolite way** opposite of to act in a respectful and polite way – **to feel contempt for sb, to despise sb** to dislike and have no respect for sb – **to gather at a funeral reception** to come together somewhere to talk and eat after a funeral – **jumper cables** electrical wires to connect batteries of two cars if one battery is dead – **to mourn (for sb)** to feel sad that sb has died and to express this in public – **to go to confession, confess your sins** to admit in church to a priest that you have done evil, and you ask for forgiveness – **to have a birth ceremony** to perform ritual acts for a newborn baby – **to (not) feel at ease** to feel (un)comfortable – **to be submissive** to be willing to do what other people tell you to do without arguing or disputing

2. Viewing comprehension

Complete the following sentences.

a. *The Kowalski family is in church because* ... _____

b. *The sons are worried about their father because* ... _____

c. *Walt does not want any help from his son or his granddaughter since* ... _____

d. *When the grandsons sneak around in Walt's basement they find* ... _____

e. *The priest asks Walt to come to confession because* ... _____

f. *Walt feels bothered by Thao because* ... _____

g. *In the garage Ashley asks Walt for two things:* ... _____

h. *Walt shows deep contempt for his Hmong neighbors by calling them* ... _____

i. *The Hmong have a family gathering in order to* ... _____

3. Analysis: Walt and Thao in their familes

a. *The two main protagonists, Walt Kowalski and Thao van Lor, are introduced in the context of their families and friends. Note and compare what you learn about them in this opening sequence.*

Finally, summarize any obvious similarities and differences between these two male protagonists.

	Walt	Thao
Description of their family (outer appearance, behavior)		
Religious traditions/ ceremonies and their reactions towards them		
Behavior/actions: what they say and do		
How the others see them		
How they seem to feel		
Similarities		
Differences		

b. *Decide where to place each protagonist on a scale of 1 to 10. "1" means a very strong feeling of alienation from family and community; "10" means: very deep sense of belonging towards family/community.*
Compare results and justify your choices. Discuss reasons for the protagonists' behavior and states of mind.

Walt:

1 -- 5 -- 10

Thao:

1 -- 5 -- 10

4. Analysis: Slipping into someone's skin

Find a partner. One focuses on Walt, the other on Thao. Pick a scene that is especially emotional for your character. Write down his thoughts in the thought bubble (circa 50 words). Afterwards, exchange texts and guess which moment your partner picked. Discuss why you each chose this exact moment.

> **Useful words:** upset – disappointed – sad – frustrated – humiliated – proud – ashamed –
> desperate – anxious – frightened – furious – shocked – worried – nervous

5. Conclusion: Their sense of belonging

Walt's sense of belonging	Thao's sense of belonging

Summarize Walt's and Thao's respective senses of belonging as expressed in this first sequence.

The Ambiguity of Belonging: The gangs (00:12:40 – 00:17:21)

1. Chunk box

> **to harass sb (verbally/sexually)** to keep annoying sb in an offensive and intrusive way – **to offend sb, to be offensive towards sb** to insult sb, to hurt sb's feeling(s) – **to fly solo** (slang) ↔ **to be tight with sb** to be on your own and not belong to a group – **"we're coz"** (slang) we're cousins, we're family – **to convince sb to do sth** to talk to sb about sth so they believe it's right (überzeugen) – **to persuade sb to do sth** to talk sb into doing sth although it's maybe wrong (überreden) – **to possess great power of persuasion** to have the ability to persuade or convince sb – **in mint condition (e.g. a car)** in excellent shape, looks like new

2. Viewing comprehension

Tick the correct statement(s). More than one statement can be correct.

1. The Mexican gang members offend Thao by

☐ laughing at his typically Asian features.

☐ making fun of his name (a girl's).

☐ teasing him for being as short and light as a girl.

☐ ridiculing him for his feminine looks.

2. After chasing the Mexican gang, the Hmong gang tries to persuade Thao to get in the car

☐ by offering him money.

☐ by threatening to kill him with the gun.

☐ by saying that he must be thankful for their help.

☐ by promising him a girlfriend.

3. When the Hmong gang shows at the house,

☐ we find out how old Sue is.

☐ we learn what Spider's real name is.

☐ we get that Smokie is Thao's cousin.

☐ we realise that Thao is already 18.

3. Analysis: The gang's powers of persuasion

a. *Read the film dialogue closely. Analyze the verbal strategies the gang uses to persuade Thao to join them.*

SMOKIE   Hey, you wanna roll with us, man?

SPIDER   Dude.

SMOKIE   Come on, ride with us. Come on.

SPIDER   Come on, chill with us. You need somebody to protect you, man. That's what your big coz is for.

SMOKIE   Look, dawg. I been there, and I seen it, man. Back in the day, everybody used to wanna beat me up, dawg. But now look. Nobody wanna fuck with me. Come on, let's go.

SPIDER   We're coz, right?

SMOKIE   Come on.

SPIDER   We're coz, right? We're family.

SMOKIE   Look, a brother to Spider is a brother to me. Come on.

SPIDER   Dude man, take this shit off. Come on.

SMOKIE   Come on, roll with us. Come on.

SPIDER   That's a woman's work.

SMOKIE   Come get your hands dirty, man.

[**dawg** – (*slang*) close friend]

b. *Re-watch the scene (00:16:06 – 0:16:42). How do Spider/Smokie use their bodies to put pressure on Thao?*

c. *Analyze the effects of camera angles/field size that underline the verbal and physical pressure Thao feels.*

Camera technique	Effect
Camera angle	
Field size	
Other techniques	

4. Analysis: Thao's ambivalence

a. *Thao is torn between "flying solo" and "rolling with the gang". Imagine two voices in his head. Make a list of reasons for i) staying away from them, and ii) joining them.*

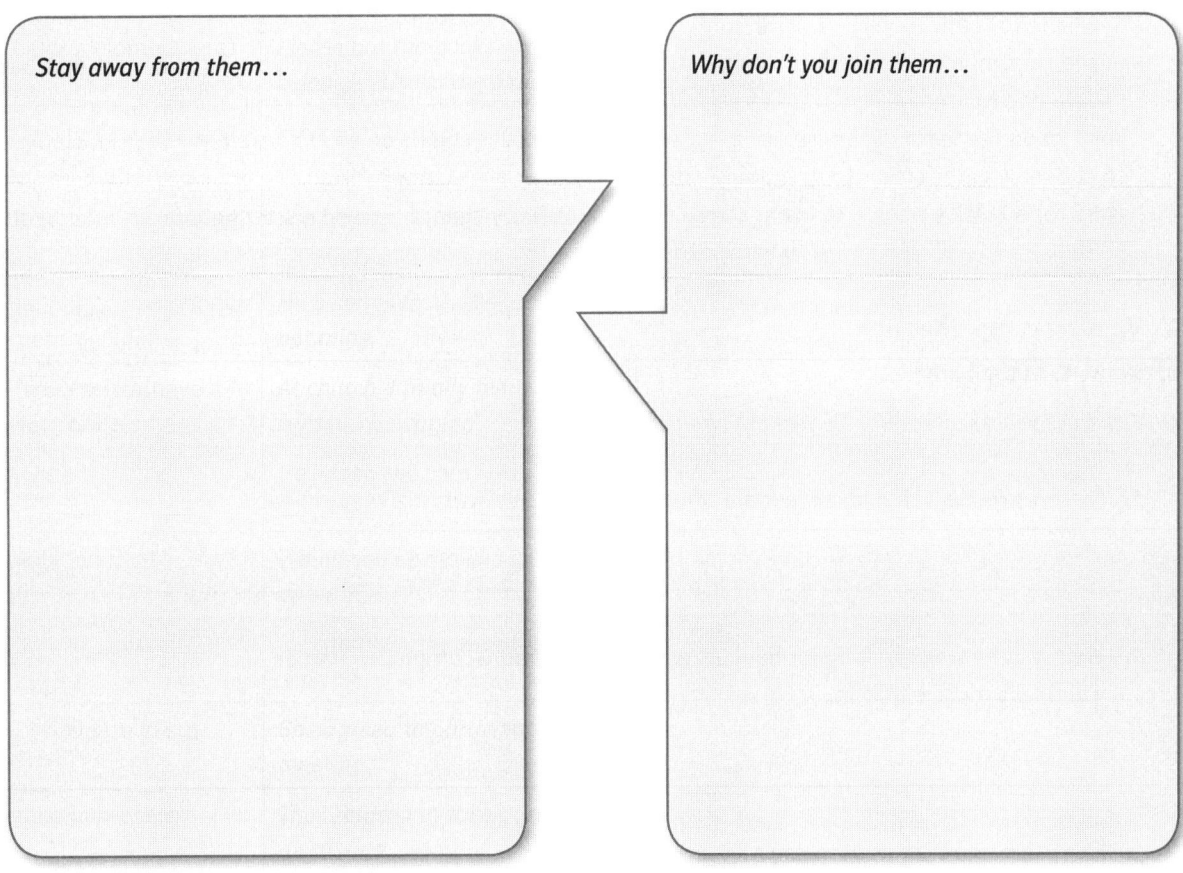

Stay away from them…

Why don't you join them…

b. *Compare your ideas with a partner and decide which voice is stronger.*

5. Conclusion: Thao's lack of belonging

Explain why Thao is an ideal "victim" for a gang (just like many other young Hmong men).

_____

_____

_____

_____

_____

_____

_____

_____

_____

_____

The Ambiguity of Belonging: Language (00:30:22 – 00:38:33)

1. Chunk box

> **to banter (with sb)** to tease/make fun of each other in an affectionate way – **a cheap person** sb who is unwilling to spend money – **a prick** *(offensive/vulgar)* highly insulting word for a man (prick = *Penis*) – **hard-nosed** uncompromising, tough – **to keep the change** *das Wechselgeld behalten* – **to hang out in a bad/ unsafe neighborhood** *sich in einem schlechten/unsicheren Viertel rumtreiben* – **mouthy** rude, impolite – **to keep sb on the leash** *jdn an der Leine führen* – **to put a chain/chains on sb** *jdn anketten* – **to yank sb** to pull sb suddenly with force – **to quit doing sth** to stop doing sth – **spook** *(offensive and racist)* offensive hate word for a black person – **to come across sb** to meet sb by chance – **wrinkles, wrinkly** *(Haut)falten, faltig* – **"Shut your face!"** *(informal)* "Halt die Schnauze!"

2. Viewing comprehension

a. Scene 1: At the barber's

Tick the correct sentence(s). Correct the wrong ones.

1. Martin says Walt should come more often because his haircuts are really cheap. ☐

_____

2. Walt says he waits so long for haircuts as he hopes a more competent barber will finally replace Martin. ☐

_____

3. Five years ago Walt used to pay 10 dollars for a haircut. ☐

_____

4. Walt says that he won't wait for three weeks to get his next haircut. ☐

_____

b. Scene 2: At the street corner

Put the statements into the correct chronological order. One statement is incorrect and must be crossed out.

_____ Sue is not intimidated, bravely defends herself.   _____ The gang acts in a defensive way.

_____ The gang feels provoked and threatens Trey.   _____ Trey courageously tries to protect Sue.

_____ The gang ridicules Walt because of his age.   _____ One of the African-Americans sexually harasses Sue with words and gestures.

_____ The gang doesn't know how to deal with Sue and becomes physically aggressive.   _____ Trey pretends to be one of the gang members.

3. Analysis: Signs of belonging (00:30:43 – 00:34:36)

a. *Watch the two scenes closely. Analyze the conventions or "codes" used that establish a sense of belonging to a group (e.g. dress code, specific language, gestures). In each scene, 1 and 2, focus on:*

	scene 1: **Walt and Martin**	scene 2: **The African-American gang members**
Note down similarities in the outer appearance, body language and gestures between the people		
Note phrases and describe the language that the people use to show that they belong to a person or a group		
What does this "code" reveal about the kind of relationship the people have?		

b. *Compare your results with your own experience: Do you also share different languages or codes with certain people or groups, which underline your sense of belonging to them?*

4. Analysis: Freeze frames

Find a partner (or two). Pick a scene that you think expresses "belonging" or "not-belonging" especially well. Then:

1. *Prepare a freeze frame to capture this moment.*

2. *Animate your freeze frame: Each student develops one gesture or movement out of his or her position.*

3. *In a last step add a short sentence to your gesture.*

Present your portrayal in three steps:

1. freeze frame; 2. freeze frame+movement; 3. freeze frame + movement + sound

5. Conclusion: Sense of belonging

Summarize the influence of language and other "codes" on our sense of belonging or lack thereof.

The Ambiguity of Belonging: Walt's birthday   (00:38:34 – 00:46:43)

1. Chunk box

> **1. She drops her grocery bags. 2. "Can we just drop it?"** 1. She lets her grocery bags fall on the ground. 2. "Can we just stop doing it/talking about it?" – **to maintain sth (a house/a vehicle/a road)** to keep sth in a good condition (by repairing it) – **to mow the lawn** to cut grass (in a yard or a park) – **to shovel snow** to use a shovel to remove snow from a pathway – **to be alert** to be able to think in a clear way – **to benefit from (doing) sth** to profit from (doing) sth – **old people's home, retirement home** *Altersheim, Seniorenheim* – **"I'm (just) kidding."** *(colloquial)* "I'm not serious!"/"I don't mean it seriously!" – **After all, it is** my birthday. *Immerhin/schließlich habe ich Geburtstag.* – **to yell at sb, to be yelled at** to shout at sb, to be shouted at – **to express embarrassment** to show that you feel embarrassed (*peinlich*) – **to come back for seconds** to come back to help oneself to more food – **a shaman** ['ʃɑːmən] a priest-like person who can cure illnesses – **to have no flavor** to not taste like anything – **gook** very offensive word for sb from Asia

2. Viewing comprehension

Take notes to answer the following questions. Make two points for each question.

1. What does Walt's horoscope say?

_____

_____

2. Why does Walt get so angry at Mitch and Karen's presents and suggestions?

_____

_____

3. What arguments does Sue use to persuade Walt to come over to the barbecue?

_____

_____

4. What Hmong rules of conduct (i.e. rules of how to behave) does Walt learn from Sue?

_____

_____

5. What does Kor Khue, the shaman, "read" in Walt?

_____

_____

EXTRA: With a partner, agree on a German translation for the proverb "When in Rome, do as the Romans do." Explain its meaning (possibly with examples of your own experience) and relate it to the barbeque scene.

3. Analysis: "Happy Birthday"

a. *Make a "graph of loneliness" for Walt. Discuss your results with your neighbour, justify your assessment.*

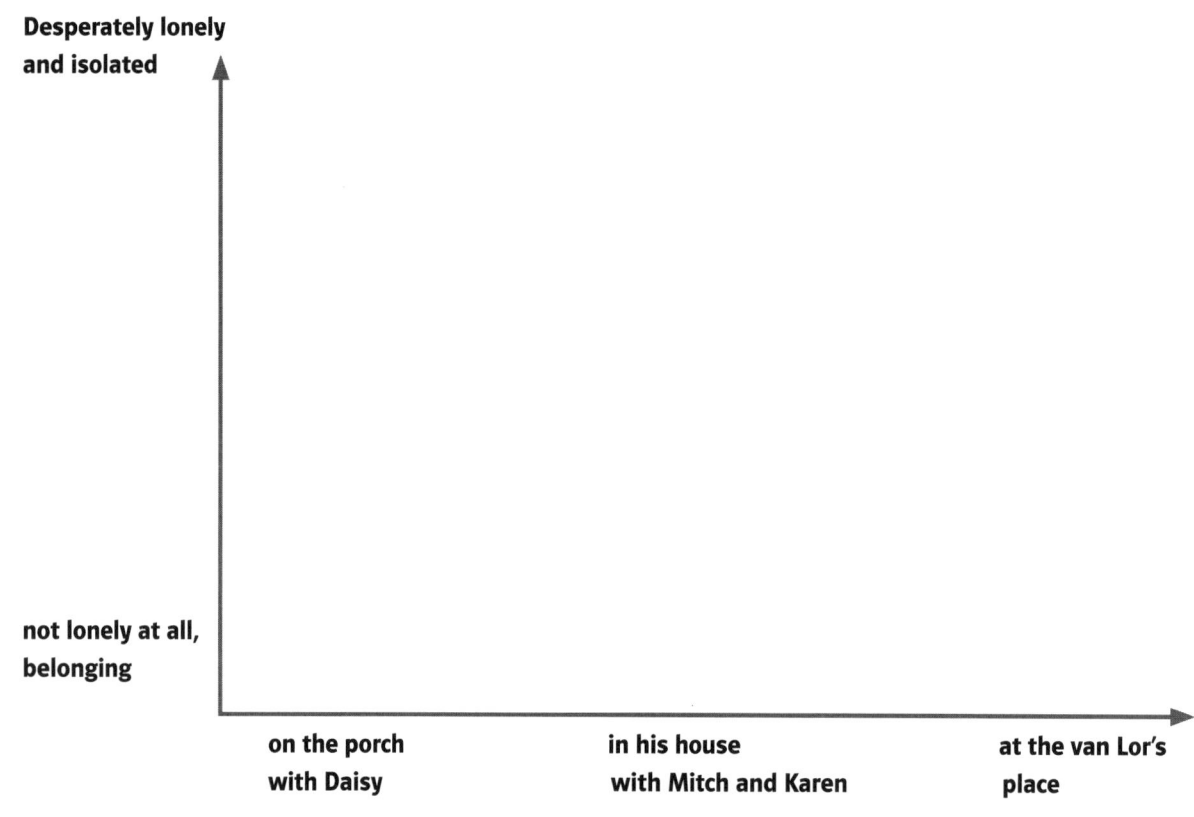

**Desperately lonely
and isolated**

**not lonely at all,
belonging**

| on the porch | in his house | at the van Lor's |
| with Daisy | with Mitch and Karen | place |

b. *Analyze Walt's change of heart on his birthday when he overcomes his prejudices against the Hmong "barbarians". Why does he suddenly respect/admire them? Think of these elements and their relationships:*

Sue   The shaman   The Hmong people

WALT

Thao   Food/drinks

4. Analysis: The mirror moment

> *And since you know you cannot see yourself*
> *So well as by reflection, I your glass*
> *Will modestly discover to yourself*
> *That of yourself which you yet know not of.*
>
> **William Shakespeare, Julius Caesar, Act I, scene 2**

a. *The mirror is a widespread symbol in literature and film. It can be a symbol of:*

- physical reflection, showing how we currently appear;
- inner reflection and self-evaluation, reflecting upon our thoughts and our identity;
- a character's duality (dark/bright side);
- prophecy foreshadowing the future.

Discuss what meaning(s) the mirror has in Walt's mirror scene.

b. *Write an extension of Walt's mirror moment, in which he reflects on his birthday, explaining his new insights.*

_____

_____

_____

_____

> "God, I've got more in common with these gooks than I have with my own spoilt, rotten family. Jesus Christ …
> Happy Birthday."

_____

_____

_____

_____

_____

5. Conclusion: Sense of belonging

Assess Walt's growing sense of alienation to his family and growing sense of belonging to the Hmong people.

_____

_____

_____

_____

_____

The Ambiguity of Belonging: Thao's initiations (01:10:06 – 01:16:46)

1. Chunk box

initiation process or ceremony in which sb becomes accepted by a group or society – **rite of passage** ceremony or event that marks a decisive stage in sb's life, e.g. becoming an adult or member of a religious group, etc. – **zipperhead** (*offensive*) highly offensive word for sb from Asia, which may go back to the Korean war, when US jeeps ran over Asian enemy soldiers. The tires sometimes left patterns that looked like a zipper (*Reißverschluss*) on the dead bodies. – **toad** 1. *Kröte* 2. Offensive word for a stupid person – **to blow sth** (*informal*) *etwas vermasseln* – **to gather sth** here: to think/assume sth – **to talk sb into doing sth** to persuade sb to do sth – **to banter (back and forth) with sb** to speak in a playful and teasing way with sb – **to vouch for sb/sth** *für jdn/etwas bürgen/einstehen* – **to be totally/really into (doing) sth** to like (doing) sth and be convinced of it – **You bet!** (*spoken*) Of course! – **You owe me one!** (*spoken*) *Du schuldest mir was!*

2. Reading comprehension

a. Read the texts and locate them. Find their setting, context, what happened before and what will happen next.

Text 1
GRAND: I'm just so broken-hearted. I want my daughter to find another husband. If she married again, there would be a man in the house.
MAN: What about Thao? The man of the house is right there.
GRAND: Look at him washing dishes. He does whatever his sister orders him to do. How could he ever become the man of the house?
MAN: Be patient, once he's older, he will be the man of the house.
GRAND: No way.

Text 3
WALT: So… what exactly was the deal with those guys out on my lawn that night? Who are they?
THAO: A gang. Hmong gangbangers.
WALT: I gathered that. What did they want with you?
THAO: They wanted to take me away because I blew my first initiation.
WALT: You joined up with those pukes? Damn, you are a pussy. Why in the hell did you do that?
THAO: I don't know. They were persuasive. My cousin's in the gang. They just talked me into it I guess.
WALT: Well, at least you're honest about it. So how'd you blow your first initiation?
Thao nods towards the Gran Torino.
WALT: The Gran Torino?
Thao nods. Walt laughs.
WALT: Christ all Friday.

Text 2
WALT: Relax, zipperhead. I am not gonna shoot you. I'd look down too if I was you. You know, I knew you were a dipshit the first time I ever saw you. You're worse with women than you are with stealing cars, Toad.
THAO: Thao.
WALT: What?
THAO: It's not toad, it's Tao. My name is Tao.
WALT: You were blowing it with that girl who was there. Not that I give two shits about you, Toad.
THAO: You don't know what you are talking about.
WALT: You are wrong, egg roll. I know exactly what I am talking about. I may not be the most pleasant person to be around. But I got the best woman who was ever on this planet to marry me. I had to work at it. That was the best thing that ever happened to me. Hands down. But you … you know. You let Click Clack, Ding Dong and Charlie Chan just walk out with what's-her-face. She likes you, you know. Though I don't know why.
THAO: Who?
WALT: Yum Yum! You know that girl in the purple sweater. She's been looking at you all day, stupid.
THAO: Do you mean, Youa?
WALT: Yeah, Yum Yum. Yeah. Nice girl, very charming girl. I talked with her. But you let her just walk right out. With the three stooges. And you know why? Cause you are big, fat pussy. Well …I gotta go. Good day. Puss cake.

b. Thao failed the first gang initiation (stealing the Gran Torino). What might Thao's next initiations be?

3. Analysis: The language test (01:10:06 – 01:15:38)

a. Watch the two scenes with Walt and Thao, first at the barber's shop and then at Mr. Kennedy's office. Use the grid to take notes on the rules Walt teaches Thao in the first scene and tick off (b) the ones that Thao actually follows in the second scene. Analyze your findings: Has Thao passed the test?

How to talk like real men:

Do's

Don'ts

b. Their language is full of extremely offensive, racist, vulgar expressions. Give some examples and explain why the friends deliberately use such offensive language (they obviously do not intend to insult each other).

4. Analysis: From Toad to Thao

a. From dishwasher to owner of a Gran Torino. Make four snapshots to illustrate Thao's steps towards manhood. If you don't like drawing, write short descriptions of the snapshots.

b. Swap results with a partner, who should identify the scenes. Compare and justify your choices.

c. Discuss whether Walt's initiation into manhood for Thao has been successful and if manliness means the same for Americans and for the Hmong. Has he finally become "the man of the house" of the Hmong family, a role his grandmother did not consider him capable of at the beginning of the movie?

5. Conclusion: Sense of belonging

Summarize Thao's development and his ambivalence of standing in between boyhood and manhood.

The Ambiguity of Belonging:
Walt's confession & atonement

(01:32:33 – 01:37:25)

1. Chunk box

> **to go to confession** *zur Beichte gehen* – **to absolve sb from one's sins** *jdn von seinen Sünden freisprechen* – **to make amends for sth** *etwas wiedergutmachen* – **to atone for one's sins** *für seine Sünden büßen* – **as atonement for sth** *als Wiedergutmachung für etwas* – **a confessional with a latticed window** *ein Beichtstuhl mit einem Gitterfenster* – **to retaliate against sb for sth** *sich bei jdn für etwas rächen* – **Not a day goes by that I don't think about it.** *Kein Tag vergeht, an dem ich nicht daran denke.* – **to lock sb up in the basement** *jdn im Keller einschließen* – **to be soiled** to be unclean, here: to have sinned – **We've come a long way.** We have achieved many things – **You've got your whole life <u>ahead</u> of you.** *Du hast dein ganze Leben vor dir.*

EXTRA: Explain the use of the present perfect in these sentences.

"What have you done?"	"How long has it been since your last confession?"
"Bless me, Father, for I have sinned."	"It's bothered me most of my life."

What tense do you expect Walt to use in his confession? Why?

2. Viewing comprehension

Take notes. What does Walt confess to Father Janovich in church and to Thao in the basement?

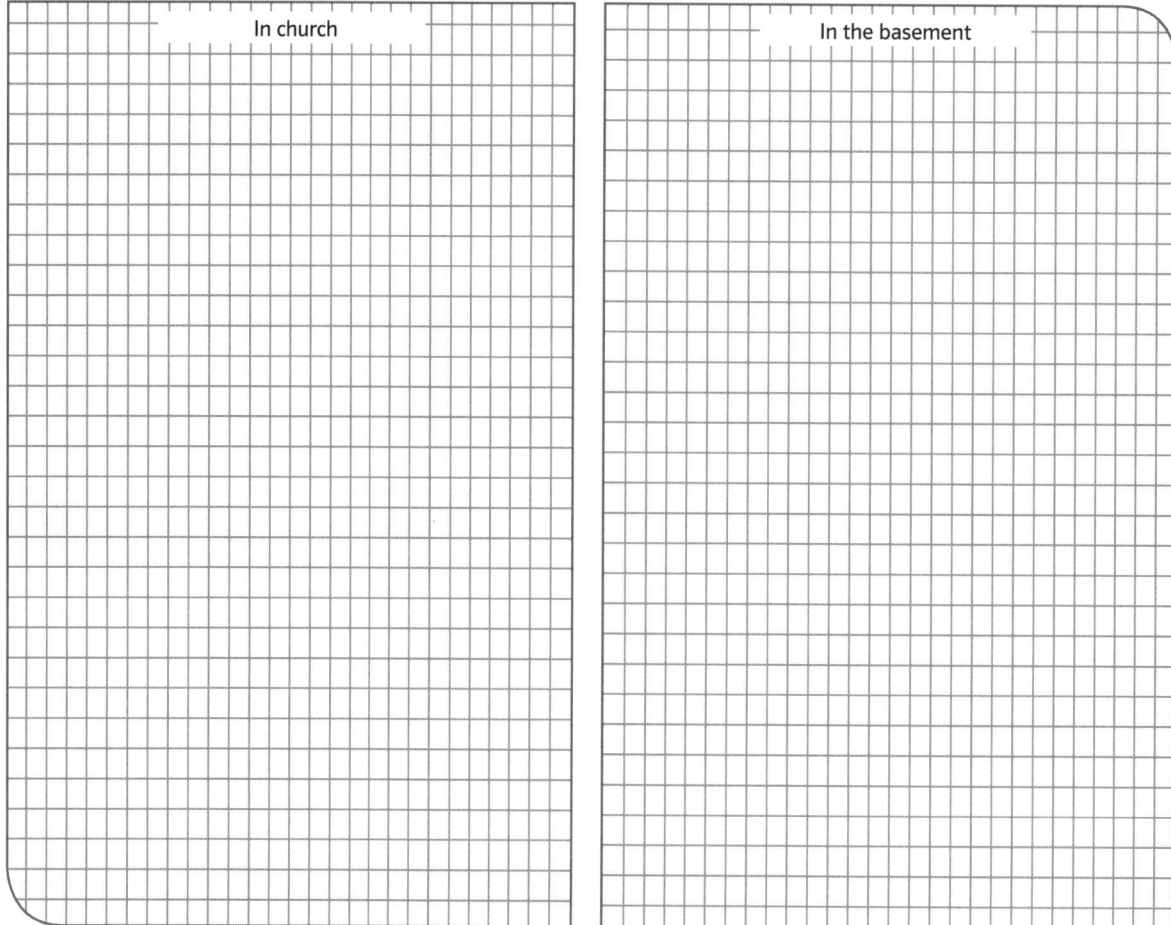

In church

In the basement

EXTRA: Compare the content, the setting and the characters in the two confessions.

3. Analysis

a. *Which statement(s) do you agree with? Which do you disagree with? Point out your strongest arguments.*

Walt goes to confession because:
1. ... it had been his wife's wish.
2. ... he has regained confidence in the church through Father Janovich.
3. ... he seeks forgiveness for his sins through Jesus Christ.

b. "The thing that haunts a man the most is what he <u>isn't</u> ordered to do." *(Walt to Father Janovich)*

Explain Walt's statement. Outline how he finally makes up (atones) for these past mistakes:

Past mistakes that burden Walt	How Walt makes up for them in the movie
i) He has never had a close relationship with his sons.	
ii) He killed a teenager in Korea, although he had surrendered.	
iii) He intensified the gang conflict, including the drive-by shooting and Sue's brutal rape.	

4. Analysis: Being at peace

"He says: 'You have no happiness in your life. It's like you are not at peace.'" *(Sue translating the Shaman's words for Walt)*… "I am at peace." *(Walt to Father Janovich after his confession)*

a. Explain what it means (not) "to be at peace". You can refer to your own experience.

b. Imagine Walt writes a note to Thao and Sue on the day he dies. He tells them how their friendship has finally brought him peace and light and explains his plan to defeat the Hmong gang to them. Write this note.

5. Conclusion: Sense of belonging

Outline Walt's development towards a feeling of belonging in the sense of self-acceptance and inner peace.

The Ambiguity of Belonging: Walt's will

(01:45:25 – 01:51:47)

1. Chunk box

> **to deliver/give a eulogy** to give a speech at a funeral about the person who died – **to make/write a (last) will (and testament)** to create a legal document that states what you want to happen to your money and belongings after you die – **to leave sb sth/to bequeath** [bɪˈkwiːθ] **sth/to hand down sth to sb** to (say that you) leave sb sth after your death – **to inherit sth from sb** to receive sth from sb who has died – **to receive an inheritance from sb** to get money or possessions from sb who has died – **to leave sb a legacy** *ein (materielles oder ideelles) Erbe hinterlassen* – **cultural heritage** traditions and beliefs that are part of the history and culture of a group – **along the lakeshore** following the banks/shore of a lake – **to sit in the passenger seat** to sit in the front seat next to the driver – **to head for/to** to go in a certain direction or to a certain place – **Where are you headed?** Where are you going? What's your destination? – **lighthouse** tower with a flashing light that tells ships where they are

2. Viewing comprehension

a. *Walt leaves his Gran Torino to Thao in his will, but only conditionally. Name at least two of the conditions.*

_____

_____

_____

_____

_____

b. *Choose the best adjective(s) to describe Walt's language from the notary's point of view (left side) and from Thao's point of view (right side). EXTRA: Justify and explain your assessment.*

Notary		Thao
☐	ironic	☐
☐	formal	☐
☐	offensive	☐
☐	intimate	☐
☐	vulgar	☐

_____

_____

_____

_____

_____

3. Analysis: Walt's last will and testament

a. *Rank the characters present at the notary in order of status (in relation to everyone else). Who has (or <u>thinks</u> they have) the highest/lowest status (from 1–6) at the <u>beginning</u> and who at the <u>end</u>? Explain your choices.*

	Beginning	End
Notary	☐	☐
Thao van Lor	☐	☐
Mitch Kowalski (Walt's oldest son)	☐	☐
Karen Kowalski (Mitch's wife)	☐	☐
Ashley Kowalski (Mitch and Karen's daughter)	☐	☐
Steve Kowalski (Walt's younger son)	☐	☐

b. *Discuss what kind of ranking or hierarchy this is. Does the status depend on the character's ethnicity, social class, profession, age or maybe something else?*

c. *Analyze the film techniques used to emphasize the change in Thao's ranking (e.g. picture composition (where is he positioned?); lighting; field size; other aspects).*

– Composition _____

_____

– Lighting _____

_____

– Field size _____

_____

EXTRA: One aspect of *post-production editing* is putting the different shots and sequences of the movie together, called *cutting*. The most common cut is the *hard cut*, where one shot ends and the next one starts immediately. But the transition from the notary scene to the final Gran Torino scene is made with a *dissolve*. Watch this transition (cut) at least twice. Describe what a *dissolve* is and what function it has (why did the editor NOT choose a hard cut?). Stop in the middle of the dissolve and analyze the effect it produces.

Description	Function	Effect

4. Analysis: Gentle now a tender breeze blows

a. *Describe Thao's state of mind in the final scene. Which emotions do you consider to be most dominant?*

sad – loved – confused – optimistic – alone – self-confident – safe – proud – in the right place

Visualize your findings by creating a hand-written "wordle", in which the size of the letters indicates the intensity of the feeling. You can find numerous examples of wordles on the internet (picture search).

b. *In the scene there is a strong sense of belonging between Walt and Thao, even though Walt is dead. Analyze the techniques used to emphasize the bond between these two unusual friends. What symbols are used? What effect does the music (mood, voice) have?*

c. *Read quotes from Jamie Cullen's theme song "Gran Torino" and/or listen to it. The bittersweet ballad, sung by Clint Eastwood, revolves around themes from the movie.*

"So tenderly your story is
nothing more than what you see
or what you've done or will become."

"standing strong do you belong
in your skin; just wondering."

"Gentle now a tender breeze blows
whispers through the Gran Torino
whistling another tired song."

"Engines hum and bitter dreams grow
a heart locked in a Gran Torino
it beats a lonely rhythm all night."

"Realign all the stars above my
head."

"I drink instead on my own Oh!
how I've known
the battle scars and worn out beds.
[…]"

"May I be so bold and stay
I need someone to hold
[…]"

"Engines hum and better dreams
grow."

Match themes from the box with the song lyrics and explain your decisions. Add more themes if you can.

self-acceptance – self-judgment – self-reflection – old age – loneliness – nostalgia – haunting memories – the need to belong – affection – exhaustion – hope – change – regrets – endurance – tranquility

5. Conclusion: Sense of belonging

Summarize the significance of the contents of Walt's will. Assess what they reveal about Walt's sense of belonging, and analyze the effect it has on Thao's sense of belonging.

Walt's sense of belonging	Thao's sense of belonging

The Ambiguity of Belonging: Walt's development

"Dad's still living in the 50s." (Walt's son Steve)

a. *Walt Kowalski is a fossil, out of place in a world where everything (objects, people, values) has changed or deteriorated. Describe Walt's present life (at the beginning of the movie) in contrast to his past life.*

	Walt's past life	Walt's present life (beginning of the movie)
Historical background	Detroit in the 1950s: peak population of 1.8 million; well-paid jobs in the automobile industry	Detroit in the 21st century: decline of the auto industry, unemployment, dramatic drop in population, entire neighborhoods are abandoned
His house/his neighbourhood/ his community	well-maintained house in a safe neighbourhood where mostly white middle-class people/automobile workers lived; he went to church because it was important to his wife	
His job	worked all of his life for the Ford Motor Company assembling cars; put the steering column on his own Gran Torino	
His family	was married to the best wife he could imagine, had two sons, never had a close relationship with his sons	
His doctor	Dr. Feldman used to be his (experienced, male, white) doctor.	
War/violence/ crime	• fought as a soldier in Korea • won a Silver Medal for his service • killed people, even a teenager • lost many friends in the battle • learned to rely on himself and to defend himself.	

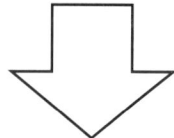

Remaining moments of warmth and belonging in Walt's present life:
- *sitting on his porch with his dog, drinking beer, admiring his Gran Torino in the driveway*
-
-
-

b. *Evaluate your findings and interpret Walt's ambiguity of belonging. Describe the ambivalence he experiences and comment on the emotional consequences it has on Walt. You can also refer to these quotes:*

[Sue translating what the Hmong shaman says about Walt:]
He says the way you live, your food has no flavor. You're wearied by your life.
You made a mistake. And your past life is like a mistake what you did. You are not satisfied with.
He says, you have no happiness in your life. It's like you are not at peace.

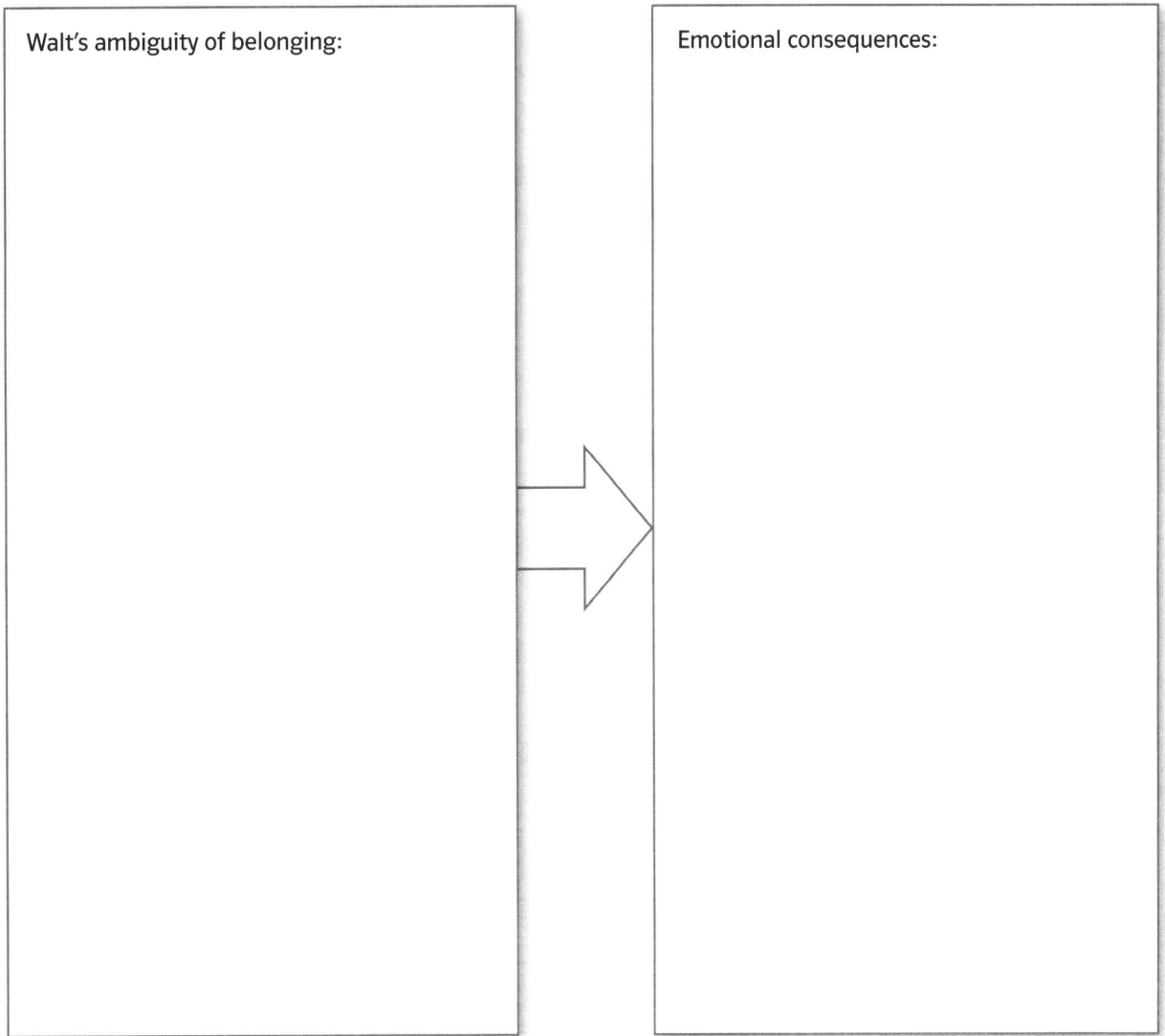

Walt's ambiguity of belonging:

Emotional consequences:

The Ambiguity of Belonging: Thao's development

> "He just doesn't know which direction to go in." (Sue)

1. Thao's lack of direction

Read through the list of possible reasons for Thao's lack of orientation at the beginning of the movie.
With your partner discuss their significance and agree on the three most important ones.

- He doesn't have a father or a male role model in his family.
- He doesn't fit into his traditional Hmong family, and yet he is seen as a suitable (future) man of the house.
- He is a boy with qualities that are commonly seen as female; he is rather submissive and introverted and lets Sue order him around. He does "women's work' in the kitchen and the yard. His name is commonly used as a girl's name.
- He doesn't go to school, has no job and no idea about what to do with his life.
- He's different from other young Hmong men in the movie (reads books, helps the old lady next door, etc.).
- He doesn't seem to have any friends (e.g. at the party he is all by himself), the only people interested in him are the Hmong gangbangers.

2. Thao's ambiguity of belonging: Boy or men? Hmong or American?

a. *Analyze Thao's outer appearance, his behaviour and how other people treat him in the course of the movie.*
What aspects make him appear like a boy or a young man, like a Hmong or like an American?

Thao, the boy	Thao, the young man

The Hmong Thao	The American Thao

b. *Summarize your findings and describe Thao's development. Examine if or how Thao finally reaches some sense of belonging.*

V. Solutions to all Language Worksheets

KV A1.L: Excel in language: Prejudices and racism

1. 1. racism 2. racist (noun) 3. racist (adjective) 4. racial 5. race relations 6. race riots 7. racial profiling
2. a. – c. against (c: "about" geht auch); d. + e. to

KV A2.L: Excel in language: Masculinity

1. Adjectives commonly associated with masculinity: ambitious, aggressive, rebellious, self-confident, active, forceful, protective, individualistic, non-emotional, tough-skinned, competitive, independent, athletic, dominant. (Neu: active)
Adjectives commonly associated with femininity: dependent, emotional, accepting, submissive, graceful, flirtatious, nurturing, self-critical, passive, sensitive, understanding, tender, vulnerable. (Neu: supportive)
2. to rise to a challenge; to offer sb protection/ safety/ one's strength; to take revenge on sb; to provide safety to sb/ sb protection/ the father role for sb; to adopt the father role for sb; to demonstrate one's strength; to suppress one's emotions; to use violence/ one's strength against sb.

KV A3.L: Excel in language: Gran Torino

1. 1. Oldtimer 2. ein fantastisches/ wunderschönes/ glänzendes Auto 3. in perfektem Zustand sein 4. in ein Auto einsteigen 5. die Türe zuschlagen 6. in einem Auto davonfahren 7. die Reifen quietschen lassen 8. ein Fahrzeug fährt an einer Stelle/ einem Ort vor 9. ein Starthilfekabel an eine leere Batterie klemmen 10. + 11. Eigene Antworten.
2. 1. Do you promise to drive carefully? – To control a vehicle (as a driver) well. 2. Stop driving yourself so hard. – To make someone work or try very hard. 3. She drove him to the airport. – To take someone to a place in a vehicle. 4. You're driving me up the wall. – To make someone extremely angry. 5. They were driven out of their village. – To force someone to leave a place.
3. a. Road, Street, Boulevard (in an address) b. hard drive (Laufwerk in einem PC) c. the desire to be successful and good at everything (Tatendrang/ Schwung) d. Drang, Triebe, instinct e.g. sex(ual) drive

KV A4.L: Excel in language: Violence

Individuelle Lösungen

KV A5.L: Excel in language: Religion

1. zur Beichte gehen 2. jdm/ einem Priester seine Sünden beichten 3. seine Schuld zugeben 4. etwas wiedergutmachen 5. seine Last/ Sünden zurücklassen 6. jdn von seinen Sünden freisprechen 7. Erlösung finden 8. Er würde sich im Grab rumdrehen, wenn er sehen könnte, dass… 9. das Vaterunser 10. "Im Namen des Vaters, des Sohnes und des Heiligen Geistes" 11. vom Leben und dem Tod predigen 12. Gottesdienst.

More expressions: to pray for sb/ sth, to go to church, to believe in God, to be religious/ pious, resurrection

KV B5: Ambiguity of belonging: Language of belonging

1. Das Nicht-wissen-wo-man-hingehört, die Ambivalenz des Dazugehörens, die ambivalente Zugehörigkeit

2. The center or root of the word 'belonging' is 'longing', which is a synonym for 'want'.
   Adjectives: e.g. a deep, desperate, great, intense, overwhelming, passionate, terrible, wild, sudden, hopeless, nostalgic, physical, sexual … longing
   Collocations: be filled with … ; be full of … ; feel/have a longing to do sth; his longing for sth

3. **Ambiguity** ~ incertitude, vagueness, double meaning, uncertainty, doubtfulness, enigma, obscurity, unclearness. **Belonging** ~ kinship, affinity, attachment, loyalty, relationship, inclusion, acceptance, association. Odd ones out: transition, challenge

4.

to belong (somewhere)	*hingehören (an einen Ort)*
to belong to sb	*jdm gehören*
to belong to sth	*zu etw. dazugehören, Mitglied sein*
to belong to sb/ sth	*zu einer Gruppe dazugehören*
to feel a sense of belonging/ to have a feeling of belonging	*eine Zugehörigkeitsgefühl haben/ spüren*
to belong to sb/ sth	*einem Verein/ einem Club beitreten*
to join sb for sth	*mit jemandem etwas zusammen machen*
to belong to sb	*sich mit etwas identifizieren*
to participate in sth	*bei etw. mitmachen/ an etwas teilhaben*
to take part in sth	*an etwas teilnehmen*
to be/ feel part of sth	*sich zugehörig/ als Teil von etwas fühlen*
to exclude sb from sth	*jdn von etw. ausschließen*
to be/ feel excluded from sth/ sb	sich von etw/ jdm ausgeschlossen fühlen

5. Individuelle Lösungen